CHILDREN
OF
POVERTY

Studies on the Effects of Single Parenthood, the Feminization of Poverty, and Homelessness

edited by

STUART BRUCHEY
University of Maine

A GARLAND SERIES

THE DIMINISHED ANTI-POVERTY IMPACT OF ECONOMIC GROWTH, THE SHIFT TO SERVICES, AND THE FEMINIZATION OF POVERTY

EMILY NORTHROP

GARLAND PUBLISHING, INC.
NEW YORK & LONDON / 1994

Library of Congress Cataloging-in-Publication Data

Northrop, Emily, 1955–
    The diminished anti-poverty impact of economic growth, the shift to
services, and the feminization of poverty / Emily Northrop.
        p.   cm. — (Children of poverty)
    Includes bibliographical references (p.   ).
    ISBN 0–8153–1674–7 (alk. paper)
    1. Poor women—United States. 2. Women heads of households—
United States. 3. Poverty—United States. 4. Economic assistance,
Domestic—United States. 5. United States—Economic conditions—
1945–   I. Title II. Series.
HV1445.N67   1994
305.4'086942—dc20   93–36057
                                                              CIP

Printed on acid-free, 250-year-life paper
Manufactured in the United States of America

For those who suffer poverty
despite economic growth

TABLE OF CONTENTS

INTRODUCTION

Economic growth in the United States was credited with creating substantial reductions in poverty in the decade between the mid 1940s and the mid 1950s. In the late 1950s some observers perceived a slowdown in this progress against poverty and a debate began over whether economic growth had remained a viable weapon against poverty. Under the Reagan Administration, budget cuts for numerous anti-poverty programs reflected the belief that "growth and prosperity [is] the only viable way to truly eliminate poverty."[1] Thus the debate on the reliability of economic growth at eliminating poverty remains an important contemporary issue.

Beginning in the 1960s professional economists sought to evaluate the anti-poverty effectiveness of economic growth by statistically modeling the growth/poverty relationship. However, the successful modeling of the two series leaves a critical issue unresolved. Namely, what factors determine the strength of the relationship? What makes economic growth more or less effective at reducing poverty?

---

[1]David Stockman, The Triumph of Politics, (New York: Harper & Row Publishers, 1986), 42.

1

One factor that significantly impacts the anti-poverty effect of economic growth is the rate of divorce. Divorce adds to the demographic group that has traditionally benefitted less from aggregate economic growth: the households that are headed by women. Consequently, higher rates of divorce diminish the viability of growth as instrument against poverty.

Women and the households that they head suffer higher poverty rates than the remainder of the population. Also, in the 1960s and 1970s women experienced an increasingly large portion of all poverty in the United States. This trend has been called the "feminization of poverty." However, during this period of the increased feminization of poverty, the poverty rates of women actually declined. A little reported fact is that in the early 1980s the trend toward the feminization of poverty was reversed. Thus the questions arise: What caused the feminization of poverty and why was the trend reversed? How useful is the "feminization of poverty" measure as an indication of the economic well-being of women?

A second variable that is critical to the effectiveness of economic growth at remedying poverty is the sectoral composition of growth. The recent trend away from manufacturing and towards the production of

private services has rendered aggregate growth a less
potent anti-poverty weapon. This reflects the
differences in the characteristics of the jobs found in
each sector. Jobs in the private services sectors
typically pay less per hour, and are more often part-time
and intermittent positions.

Hence the divorce rate and the composition of
economic growth are two variables which contribute to an
explanation of the recent record on poverty in the United
States. That record is summarized in Table I.1 and the
accompanying Figures I.1 and I.2. As indicated by the
number of official poor[2] and by the poverty rate, poverty
generally declined in the 1960s, held roughly constant in
the 1970s and generally rose in the 1980s through 1985.

Chapter 1 of this dissertation begins with an
examination of the background of the modern debate on the
anti-poverty impact of economic growth. The chapter then

---

[2]The "official" measure of poverty was developed by
the Social Security Administration in 1965. Once counts
of "official poverty" became available, social scientists
commonly employed the measure. In this dissertation the
official definition of poverty is also employed.

The official poverty definition is a measure of
gross money income which varies according to family size
and is annually adjusted for changes in the C.P.I. For a
complete history of the development of the official
definition of poverty, its strengths and its weaknesses,
see: Sharon Oster, Elizabeth E. Lake, and Conchita Gene
Oksman, The Definition and Measurement of Poverty,
Volume 1: A Review (Boulder: Westview Press, 1978).

Table I.1: Aggregate poverty of individuals, 1959-1985

Year	Number living below the official poverty line, in millions	Poverty rate*
1959	39.49	22.4
1960	39.85	22.2
1961	39.63	21.9
1962	38.63	21.0
1963	36.44	19.5
1964	36.06	19.0
1965	33.19	17.3
1966	28.51	14.7
1967	27.77	14.2
1968	25.39	12.8
1969	24.15	12.1
1970	25.42	12.6
1971	25.56	12.5
1972	24.46	11.9
1973	22.97	11.1
1974	23.37	11.2
1975	25.88	12.3
1976	24.98	11.8
1977	24.72	11.6
1978	24.50	11.4
1979	26.07	11.7
1980	29.27	13.0
1981	31.82	14.0
1982	34.40	15.0
1983	35.30	15.2
1984	33.70	14.4
1985	33.06	14.0

*The poverty rate is the number of poor individuals as a percentage of the entire population.

Source: Current Population Reports P-60 Series, various years.

Figure I.1: Poor individuals, 1959-1985

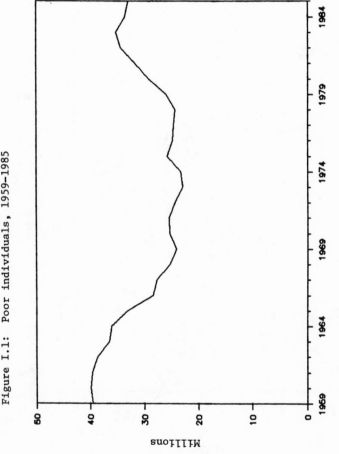

Source: Table I.1

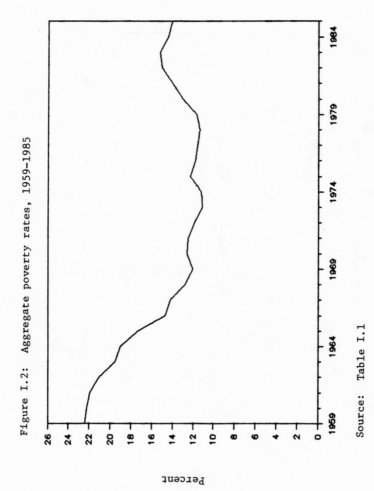

Figure I.2: Aggregate poverty rates, 1959-1985

Source: Table I.1

turns to a detailed review of the modern debate and a critique of the previous approaches to the topic.

In Chapter 2 I review the economic consequences of divorce for women and examine the extent of divorce in the United States in recent years. These considerations suggest that divorce has a significant impact on the anti-poverty viability of economic growth. Then Chapter 2 turns to a close analysis of the data which represent the poverty of women in the United States.

Chapter 3 discusses the feminization of poverty. It examines the recent trend and its causes and it critiques the usefulness of the concept as an indication of the economic welfare of women.

In Chapter 4 I turn to the second factor deemed to render economic growth less useful at combating poverty: the composition of economic growth. Also in this chapter I examine the role that women play in labor market. Finally an analysis is presented which combines the recent pattern of the composition of economic and the pattern of sex segregation in the labor market to explain the record on the feminization of poverty.

Chapter 5 concludes this study with an empirical model designed to evaluate the roles of divorce and the composition of economic growth on the anti-poverty impact of economic growth. I conclude that these variables have significantly reduced the viability of growth as an anti-poverty weapon. Finally I employ the model to anticipate the future impact of growth on poverty. Given the predicted values of divorce and the anticipated composition of industrial output, growth is expected to remain a weakened instrument against poverty.

CHAPTER 1:

ECONOMISTS' VIEWS ON THE ANTI-POVERTY

EFFECTIVENESS OF ECONOMIC GROWTH

I: Historical Background

The effects of economic growth on the welfare of the
poor have been a recurring subject for economists since
Adam Smith. Smith himself explained the low wages earned
by the industrial poor as the consequence of what he
considered an easily perceived imbalance of power between
the workers and the "masters." According to Smith, the
employers have the advantage in the wage dispute and
consequently

> ... force the [workers] into a compliance with
> their terms.   The masters, being fewer in
> number, can combine much more easily; and the
> law, besides, authorizes, or at least does not
> prohibit   their   combinations,   while   it
> prohibits those of the workmen. We have no
> acts of parliament against combining to lower
> the price of work; but many against combining
> to raise it.[1]

Smith recognized that there was a minimum below
which wages could not be reduced "for any considerable
time" lest "the   race of ... workmen could not last

---

[1]Adam Smith, The Wealth of Nations, (New York:
Penguin Books, 1970), 169.

9

beyond the first generation."[2]   Workmen must   earn enough to subsist and reproduce themselves.

Smith did offer a possible break in this dreary scenario.   He suggested that "[t]here   are certain circumstances ... which sometimes give the labourers an advantage, and enable them to raise their wage considerably above this [subsistence] rate."   It was economic growth, he believed, that offered the relief:

> When in any country the demand for those who
> live by wages, labourers, journeymen, servants
> of every kind, is continually increasing, when
> every year furnishes employment for a greater
> number than had been employed the year before,
> the workmen have no occupation to combine in
> order to raise their wages.   The scarcity of
> hands occasions a competition among masters,
> who bid against one another, in order to get
> workmen, and thus voluntarily break through the
> natural combination of masters not to raise
> wages.

He concluded:

> It is not the actual greatness of national
> wealth, but its continual increase, which
> occasions a rise in the wages of labour.   It is
> not, accordingly, in the richest countries, but
> in the most thriving, or in those which are
> growing rich the fastest, that the wages of
> labour are highest.[3]

---

[2] Ibid., 170.

[3] Ibid., 171-2.

Smith's allowance for some improvement in the plight of the working poor was replaced by the themes of Malthus and Ricardo. In particular, Malthus' theory of perpetual downward pressure on wages due to population increases that inevitably accompanied economic growth, helped establish a pessimism within Economics that led to its distinction as "the dismal science." Ricardo's "iron law of wages" contributed further to the bleak outlook. No source of substantial betterment for the vast numbers of poor via the market was again suggested until the 1940s and 1950s.[4]

II: The Beginning of the Modern Discussion: Galbraith and Harrington

The events of the post World War II economic boom in the United States offered the grounds for an optimistic reappraisal. Between 1947 and 1956 median family income rose by almost three percent per year, from approximately $3900 to $5050 (1963 dollars).[5]

Writing in 1958 John Kenneth Galbraith acknowledged that "the facts are inescapable. It is the increase in

---

[4]For a summary of the intervening contributions, see John Kenneth Galbraith, The Affluent Society, (Boston: Houghton Mifflin Company, 1958), chapters IV-VI.

[5]Lowell E. Gallaway, "The Foundations of the 'War on Poverty,'" American Economic Review, vol. 55 (March, 1965), 124.

output in recent decades, not the redistribution of income, which has brought the great material increase, the well-being of the average man." However, Galbraith argued that the beneficial effects of the growing economy had been exaggerated. In his view the common perception had evolved that "[n]ot only will there be material improvement for the average man, but there will be an end to poverty and privation for all."[6]

Galbraith sought to discredit that optimism. He held that "[i]ncreasing aggregate output leaves a self-perpetuating margin of poverty at the very base of the income pyramid." He distinguished among two types of poverty that remained: "Case poverty" he related to "some characteristic of the individuals afflicted." Perhaps "mental deficiency, bad health, inability to adapt to the discipline of modern economic life, excessive procreation, alcohol, insufficient education, or ... a combination of several of these handicaps - have kept these individuals from participating in the general well-being." "Insular poverty" he held to be "[t]hat which manifests itself as an 'island' of poverty. In the island everyone or nearly everyone is poor. ... For some reason the people of the island have been frustrated by

---

[6]Galbraith, 96 and 97.

their environment." Galbraith did not detail the causes
of insular poverty. He only related it to "the desire of
a comparatively large number of people to spend their
lives at or near the place of their birth," areas "of
intrinsically limited opportunity." His perception of
the effects of economic growth on these poverties was
clear:

> The most certain thing about modern poverty is
> that it is not efficiently remedied by a
> general and tolerably well-distributed advance
> in income. Case poverty is not remedied
> because the specific individual inadequacy
> precludes employment and participation in the
> general advance. Insular poverty is not
> directly alleviated because the advance does
> not necessarily remove the specific
> frustrations of the environment to which the
> people of these islands are subject.[7]

In contrast to the previous writers, Galbraith's
discussion of economic growth and the poor did not center
on wage levels. He even went so far as to say that
"increased output eliminated the general poverty of all
who worked." Galbraith argued that poverty in the United
States had ceased to be the plight of the "average man,"
the common worker in the prospering U.S. economy, and had
remained the burden of a somewhat distinct minority of
the population, those who were ill-suited for work and

---

[7]*Ibid.*, 97, 325, 326, and 327.

those who lived in areas which were not enjoying the general economic growth. He raised an influential challenge to the view that growth would eliminate poverty. He did not expect that outcome, and in the best light, only foresaw it to "be an infinitely time-consuming and unreliable remedy."[8]

A second assault on economic growth as a cure for modern U.S. poverty was made by Michael Harrington in The Other America (1962). Harrington's emphasis was on the widespread poverty that remained even in areas that experienced economic growth. He argued that

> [i]n the midst of general prosperity, there will be types of jobs, entire areas, and huge industries in which misery is on the increase. The familiar America of high living standards moves upward; the other America of poverty continues to move downward.[9]

Although the working poor were not the exclusive concern of his book, Harrington did redirect attention toward that group. In his view the "great mass" of workers whose incomes had risen in recent decades enjoyed their prosperity not because they had unique or individual personal talents, but rather "it was a

---

[8]Ibid., 328.

[9]Michael Harrington, The Other America: Poverty in the United States (New York: Macmillan Company, 1962), 30.

question of being at the right point in the economy at the right time in history, and utilizing that position for common struggle." He held that the poor who were left behind for the most part "had been at the wrong place in the economy at the wrong moment in history." He continued:

> These were the people in the unorganizable jobs, in the South, in the minority groups, in the fly-by-night factories that were low on capital and high on labor. When some of them did break into the economic mainstream - when, for instance, the CIO opened up the way for Negroes to find good industrial jobs - they proved to be as resourceful as anyone else. As a group, the other Americans who stayed behind were not originally composed primarily of individual failures. Rather, they were victims of an impersonal process that selected some for progress and discriminated against others.[10]

In addition to the critical role played by the labor movement, Harrington posited that technological advance and the accompanying increase in productivity, propelled many in society into higher income brackets, but proved to be a menace to others. Because the new technology required higher skills and more education, its rewards fell on those who learned to work the machines and who got the expanded education. However,

---

[10]_Ibid._, 8.

[t]hose who miss out at the very start find
themselves at a new disadvantage. A generation
ago in American life, the majority of the
working people did not have high-school
educations. But at that time industry was
organized on a lower level of skill and
competence. And there was a sort of continuum
in the shop: the youth who left school at
sixteen could begin as a laborer, and gradually
pick up skill as he went along. Today the
situation is quite different. The good jobs
require much more academic preparation, much
more skill from the very outset. Those who
lack a high school education tend to be
condemned to the economic
underworld — to low-paying service industries,
to backward factories, to sweeping and
janitorial duties. If the fathers and mothers
of the contemporary poor were penalized a
generation ago for their lack of schooling,
their children will suffer all the more.[11]

Although Harrington viewed contemporary poverty

differently than did Galbraith, he agreed that economic

growth would not solve the problem. Quite the contrary,

"the other Americans are the victims of the very

inventions and machines that have provided a higher

standard for the rest of society. They are upside-down

in the economy, and for them greater productivity often

means worse jobs." In short, "[t]hese are the people who

are immune to progress."1

Concurrent with the publication of The Affluent

Society and The Other America, there emerged an often

more technical discussion of this topic to which

[11]Ibid., 12-13.

economists have continued to contribute. In general the studies within this literature sought to measure empirically the extent to which growth had reduced poverty in the past. Most of the contributors offered predictions concerning the reliability of future growth at eliminating poverty. The analytical conceptualizations of the issue varied. That variety will be illustrated in the sample of views that follows.

III: An Early Descriptive Analysis

Robert Lampman (1959)[12] undertook a specific evaluation of Galbraith's views. Lampman's approach was similar to Galbraith's in that he described the characteristics of the poor for the purpose of determining the future effectiveness of growth at eliminating poverty. However his method and his results differed substantially. Differences in method were the use of an income level to define the "low-income population," considerable use of descriptive statistics to identify specifically that population's characteristics, statistical analysis to identify factors which contributed to and distracted from the

---

[12]Robert J. Lampman, "The Low Income Population and Economic Growth," Study Paper No. 12, Joint Economic Committee, 86th Congress of the United States, 1st Session.

reduction in the number of the low-income population, and empirical projections of future numbers of low-income people.

Lampman defined a "low-income person" as one

> ... with an income equivalent to that of a member of a four-person family with total money income of not more than $2,500 in 1957 dollars. Thus an unattached individual would be classified as a low-income person if he had income under $1,157; a member of a six-person family, if his family had income under $3,236.[13]

Lampman reported that in 1957 the group of low-income persons comprised 19 percent of the population. This "low-income" threshold adjusted for 1947 prices became $2000 for a family of four. With this income cutoff he estimated that in 1947 twenty-six percent of the nation had been in the low-income group.

Lampman associated this progress with the period's rise in average income and attributed it to "part of the process of general economic growth." He further posited that

> [t]his rise in income was made possible in turn by a great shift of the labor force among occupational and industrial groups, by a rise in the number of workers per family (from 1.48 to 1.54) and by increased production per worker within occupational and industrial groups. In

---

[13]Ibid., 4.

part the latter change was due to generally
rising levels of education and occupational
skill and in part to such factors as more
capital per worker, better management, and
technological development.[14]

His own query was to identify factors over the
period that worked against and contributed to the
reduction in the percentage of low-income status people.
His method was first to project what the 1957 low-income
population would have been had it remained in character
identical to that of 1947, and simply adjusted for the
total population increase and the population changes
among the socio-economic subgroups used in his study.
Next he compared the actual 1957 low-income population to
that hypothetical 1957 low-income population. This
enabled him to establish which changes aided and which
hindered the observed reduction in the low-income
population.

Lampman's findings were that four factors led to the
observed reduction in poverty:

(1) Reduced frequency of low income in
almost every occupational and industrial group.
(Notable exceptions were agriculture, domestic
service, and finance.)

(2) Greater than proportional growth in the
numbers employed in relatively high-paying
occupations and industries, namely
professional, technical, and kindred

---

[14]Ibid., 14.

occupations, sales, skilled crafts, construction, finance, business and repair services and government.

(3) Movement out of farm residence and farm work.

(4) Increase in the number of workers per family. This was associated with a remarkable drop in the frequency of low income among three, four, and five person families.

He discerned three factors that opposed the trend:

(1) Disproportionate increases in numbers of very large and very small consumer units.

(2) Disproportionate increases in the numbers of persons aged 65 and older and a particularly striking increase in the number of unattached individuals aged 55 and older.

(3) A relative increase in the number of family heads in the Armed Forces or not employed.[15]

Lampman used several different methods to project future drops in the percentage of low-income persons. All were premised, however, on the continued effectiveness of growth at eliminating poverty that had occurred over the previous ten years. Each method predicted approximately the same results: that by the decade of 1977-87 only about 10 percent of the population would have low-income status as compared to about 20 percent at the time of his writing.

---

[15]Ibid., 23.

At this juncture Lampman challenged Galbraith's
analysis, charging that Galbraith had "misinterpreted the
low-income population in several ways." Among his
criticisms were specific issues raised concerning
"insular" and "case" poverties. In regard to insular
poverty and the lack of mobility of those afflicted,
migration was a leading factor in Lampman's view
contributing to the reduction of the low-income
population. The response to case poverty was to assert
that "some of these characteristics of persons are
moderated over time." In particular,

> ... average educational attainment levels will
> rise in future years simply because younger
> people presently have better education than
> older people. Hence, as the current generation
> of old people pass from the scene, the percent
> of persons with low educational attainment
> will fall.[16]

Lampman's analysis concluded with the concession "of
course, that some groups will not benefit from the
process of growth in the same way that others do."[17]
Among those who tend to gain less from growth are the
geographically and occupationally immobile, and those
with low education. Groups he held to be "immune" to

---

[16]Ibid., 25.

[17]Ibid., 26.

growth were people outside of the labor force, the elderly, and "consumer units ... with female heads." Although nonwhite color was considered a handicap to obtaining better paying jobs, he noted that nonwhites had shared the recent gains and would "no doubt" continue to share in the process of growth. Again the handicap of low education was anticipated to diminish over time.

Fundamentally Lampman's disagreement with Galbraith was over the nature of the then current poverty problem. Though they agreed that economic growth had substantially reduced the number of the poor, Galbraith held that those beneficial effects would not continue because the nature of the remaining poverty was different from that which had been eliminated. In Lampman's view the improvements would continue because in essence the nature of the low-income population had not changed. Those who were "immune" to economic growth at that time (1957) made up only one-third of the low-income population, and due to demographic trends would comprise no more than one-half of the poor "for many decades" to come. Consequently in Lampman's view growth would continue to be effective at reducing poverty at only a "slightly" reduced rate.

IV: Establishment of More Statistical Approaches

A second study to reference Galbraith, and additionally Harrington, was by W. H. Locke Anderson (1964).[18] Anderson's approach to the debate set a precedent that led the subsequent discussion away from an investigation of the nature and causes of poverty to an analysis of the statistical relationship between economic growth and poverty reduction.

Anderson, as Lampman, used an income level to discern the poor. His poverty criterion was that a family, regardless of size, have an income less than $3000 in 1959 prices. Acknowledging that the single standard had shortcomings, he held it to offer the "overriding virtue of simplicity."[19]

Anderson's explicit purpose was to present statistical evidence to demonstrate "that the elimination of poverty through 'trickling down' is likely to be slower and more uncertain in the future than it has been in the past." By "trickle down" Anderson meant the elimination of poverty "by economic growth within the framework of our existing system of income

---

[18]W.H. Locke Anderson, "Trickling Down: The Relationship Between Economic Growth and the Extent of Poverty Among American Families," Quarterly Journal of Economics, 78 (November, 1964).

[19]Ibid., 514.

distribution"[20] namely via the market and not through government intervention.[21]

Anderson devised the "poverty curve" to represent the relationship between the poverty rate among families and the log of median family income. The poverty curve illustrated that when median income is well below the

---

[20]Ibid., 512.

[21]The phrase "trickle down" appears to have originated with Michael Harrington. In his view

unemployment compensation, the Wagner Act, the various farm programs, [and the 'welfare state' in general was] ... designed for the middle third [of the population] in the cities, for the organized workers, and for the upper third in the country, for the big market farmers. ... Indeed, the paradox that the welfare state benefits those least who need help most is but a single instance of a persistent irony in the other America. Even when the money trickles down, even when a school is built in a poor neighborhood, for instance, the poor are still deprived. Their entire environment ... [does] not prepare them to take advantage of the new opportunity. (The Other America, 9)

It appears that "trickle down" began to gain common usage when it was picked up by Anderson in the article presently being reviewed. For Anderson and many others (including several whose work is reviewed in this chapter) the phrase came to mean the alleviation of poverty via economic growth and market activity. However, recently Harrington asserted that the idea that growth would benefit the poor was widely accepted by liberals and radicals (in the 1960s), but that this "has nothing to do with the economics of 'trickle down.'" He asserted that "trickle down" means "that the way to stimulate growth is by giving money to the rich, who will then invest it the ways that benefit the poor." See Michael Harrington, The New American Poverty, (New York: Holt, Rinehart and Winston, 1984), 143.

poverty threshold, increases in median income serve to bring fewer families out of poverty than when median income is close to the poverty cutoff. Finally, when median income is well above the poverty line, further increases again have a smaller curative effect on poverty.

Anderson's method for estimating this relationship between growth and poverty was a two step process both because his data were limited and because he suspected that growth affected demographic groups differently. First, in order to reflect poverty rates corresponding to the more extreme income levels, he disaggregated by demographic subgroups. Second, the responsiveness to growth of the subgroups' poverty was seen to also depend upon the responsiveness of each group's median income to growth in aggregate per capita income. So, those correlations were established. Then conclusions could be drawn concerning the responsiveness of each group's poverty to aggregate economic growth.

His conclusions were that only 10 percent of all poor families, i.e., the nonwhite, nonfarm families headed by a male under the age of 65, might be expected to emerge from poverty through economic growth. This group's median income was near the poverty cutoff and it had a high elasticity with respect to aggregate income.

The group which shared in advances in its median income as aggregate income increased was the white, nonfarm household headed by a male under the age of 65. However, this group had only a thin tail of its income distribution in poverty, and consequently, economic growth was not expected to significantly alleviate poverty among these people. Anderson's remaining groups-- the farm, female-headed households, and households headed by elderly persons--

> ... are to a great degree isolated from economic growth. Their median incomes are not reliably responsive to aggregate income. ... For these, income simply does not 'trickle down' directly enough to be counted upon to reduce poverty.[22]

A subsequent study by Lowell E. Gallaway (1965)[23] reached the opposite verdict on the effectiveness of growth as an anti-poverty policy. Gallaway, in the vein of Galbraith, Harrington, and Lampman, began with a brief consideration of the nature of poverty. Then, following Anderson, he engaged in a narrow statistical analysis of the correlation between aggregate growth and poverty reduction.

---

[22]Ibid., 524.

[23]Gallaway, 1965.

At the outset he hypothesized that there existed a "backwash" of American economic life which consists of "non-participants in the increasing affluence of this society." He quoted Walter Heller who argued that these individuals are left in poverty due to "illiteracy, lack of skills, racial discrimination, broken homes, and ill health - conditions which are hardly touched by prosperity and growth."[24] If the backwash was found to be large, then economic growth would not effectively remedy poverty. However, if the backwash proved to be small, then our anti-poverty attack might continue to be lead by advances in economic growth and the backwash thesis could be deemed inconsequential.

Gallaway defined the poverty cutoff for a family to be $3000 annual income in 1963 prices. Then to test the backwash thesis, both linear and nonlinear relationships between the poverty rate and economic growth were considered. Were the relationship linear, the backwash thesis would require "an intertemporal 'shift' in the parameter associated with the economic progress variable." His linear regression of a change in the poverty rate on a change in median family income from 1947-63, (first differences were used to correct for

---

[24]Ibid., 122-123.

autocorrelation), demonstrated no such shift. But it did give a very good fit (R-squared = .93) which he held "to reflect adversely on any contention that there has been some basic shift in the relationship between the extent of poverty and economic progress."[25] Hence by this model economic growth could be expected to remain a viable anti-poverty weapon.

Alternatively, the backwash thesis might be demonstrated to hold true if the relationship between growth and poverty were non-linear. Here his first regression, the log of poverty on median family income, left a cyclical pattern in the residuals that prompted him to add the unemployment rate as an independent variable. Again he obtained a good statistical fit; and he thus concluded that "the behavior of P [the poverty rate] can be explained by the levels of median family income and unemployment in the system." He used his regressions to predict future poverty rates. Depending on the assumed growth and unemployment rates, he estimated that by 1980 the poverty rate would be reduced to between 6.4 percent and 8.7 percent. Based on this result he asserted that a backwash did exist but that its size was only 6 percent. While the only route out of

_____

[25]Ibid., 127.

poverty for most of that remaining 6 percent was through direct subsidization, given the 1963 poverty rate of approximately 20 percent, great progress still could be made by relying on economic growth. Consequently, in his view, the case for selective anti-poverty programs was weakened and that "greater consideration should be given to the role which economic growth can play in eliminating poverty."[26]

A unique aspect of Gallaway's analysis was its aggregate measure of the poor. That is, no consideration was given for how the burden of the remaining poverty would fall differentially among demographic groups.

Gallaway's method and conclusions were directly challenged by Henry Aaron (1967).[27] Aaron's argument centered on three specific points. First, he demonstrated that the use of aggregate data was inappropriate in measuring the size of the backwash. He displayed a simple mathematical exercise (see Equation 1) which illustrated that one can assume a backwash, then linearly relate the aggregate poverty to median income, but then with extrapolation find the poverty rate to fall

---

[26]Ibid., 128 and 130.

[27]Henry Aaron, "The Foundations of the 'War on Poverty' Reexamined," American Economic Review, 57, (December, 1967).

below the originally assumed backwash level. Consequently, Aaron argued, to develop the backwash thesis one needs to look to the subpopulations where the thesis is most likely to apply.

$$\Delta PR = B - b\,(Y), \tag{1}$$

where PR = poverty rate;
      B = backwash;
      Y = median family income.

Second, Aaron contested Gallaway's semilogarithmic functional form. Aaron cited a Muth conclusion "that the semilogarithmic form produces estimates which overstate the rate at which increases in income will reduce the percentage of families with incomes below any constant cutoff if incomes are distributed approximately log-normally."[28] Muth had demonstrated that a double log regression would give more accurate results. As expected, Aaron's projected poverty rates exceeded Gallaway's.

Third, Aaron showed that Gallaway's optimistic results depended on his use of aggregated data. When separate regressions were run on various demographic groups, the sensitivity of poverty to economic growth and unemployment was found to vary significantly.

―――――――――――――

[28] Ibid., 1232.

In a reply to Aaron, Gallaway (1967) conceded "that the double log regression form is superior to the semi-log from the standpoint of shedding light on the relationship between poverty and economic growth in the United States." This superiority was evident both on conceptual grounds and in how well it predicted. Also Gallaway held that the significance of the backwash thesis depended on its quantitative importance, and that in light of the new evidence "it must be considered a significant thesis."[29]

In a note on Anderson's article, Perl and Solnick (1971) criticized the implicit assumption underlying Anderson's analysis that "the variance of the log of income within each subgroup is itself unaffected by the growth of income."[30] They suspected that for some subgroups the variance had diminished and consequently that Anderson had underestimated the future reduction in poverty. They were the first within this literature to test empirically the effects of growth on the dispersion of the income distribution. Specifically they regressed

---

[29]Lowell E. Gallaway, "The Foundations of the 'War on Poverty': Reply,'" American Economic Review, 57 (March, 1967), 1241 and 1242.

[30]Lewis J. Perl and Loren M. Solnick, "A Note on 'Trickling Down,'" Quarterly Journal of Economics, 85 (February, 1971), 172.

the Gini ratio of the nonwhite subgroup against the percent change in per capita income (1947-1964). Based on their findings, the income distribution for this subgroup would be expected to narrow when aggregate per capita income increases more than two percent per year.

This concern over a changing variance in the distribution of income combined with Anderson's cumbersome two-step process of analysis, prompted Perl and Solnick to estimate directly the sensitivity of each subgroup's poverty incidence to changes in per capita income for the entire population. For this purpose they modified Anderson's definition of poverty to incorporate new empirical findings of a Social Security Administration study which had reported that the poverty cutoff for farm families should be approximately 30 percent less than the $3000 cutoff for the nonfarm population. Due to the availability of data, $2000 was selected as the poverty level for farm families. Their results supported "a somewhat greater sensitivity of poverty to economic growth" than Anderson had demonstrated.[31]

---

[31] Ibid., 178.

V: Recent Studies

Thornton, Agnello, and Link, (1978; hereafter, Thornton, et al.) set out to prove Anderson's hypothesis and did conclude that trickle down had "petered out." These researchers explicitly distinguished between two fundamental issues in the analysis of growth and poverty. First is "determining the past contribution of growth to the overall reduction of poverty and establishing whether the past contribution will persist." For them a separate issue was "isolating the factors which cause some individuals to be poor."[32]   They focused exclusively on the first matter. This segregation of the issues was in sharp contrast to the earlier approaches of Galbraith, Harrington, and Lampman who sought to understand the nature of poverty in order to predict whether or not growth would alleviate it.

Thornton, et al. employed two different definitions of poverty. They first performed the analysis using a traditional absolute poverty threshold. They selected a $3,128 income threshold (in 1963 prices) which had been adopted by the federal government as the "official" poverty line applicable to a nonfarm family of four.

---

[32]James R. Thornton, et al., "Poverty and Economic Growth: Trickle Down Peters Out," Economic Inquiry, (July, 1978), 385.

The second definition of poverty was referred to as a "semi-relative" poverty definition. It had been developed by Kilpatrick and was based on public responses from 1957 through 1971 to the Gallup poll question, "What is the smallest amount of money a family of four ... needs each week to get along in this community?"

The Thornton, et al. study appears to have been the first to allow for the separate anti-poverty effectiveness of transfers. Also the selected linear functional form employed a dummy variable to directly allow for a diminished impact of growth on poverty since 1964 relative to the 1947 through 1963 period.

The results using the "semi-relative" definition of poverty indicated that during the 1964-74 decade, "economic growth did not significantly reduce the incidence of poverty for any of the nine [demographic] groups examined." The results over the same time period using the absolute definition of poverty indicated that only among two of their seven groups, namely "all families" and "male headed households," was poverty significantly reduced as a consequence of growth. Thornton, et al. claimed to have "also confirmed directly Anderson's hypothesis that the impact of growth on poverty diminishes with rising affluence." They concluded:

> The policy implications are obvious. Since
> primary reliance on future economic growth to
> reduce poverty will be largely unsuccessful,
> expanded programs directed specifically
> at poor families will be required if poverty is
> to be eliminated.[33]

A critique of Thornton, et al. was presented by Barry Hirsch (1980). Hirsch's primary concern was the use of the change in the poverty rate as the dependent variable. He argued that a change in the poverty rate from 20 percent to 10 percent ought be treated differently than a change from 10 percent to zero percent. That is, since the poverty base is shrinking, "it is hardly surprising that they find trickle down petering out."[34]

Hirsch preferred instead to treat changes in poverty from 20 percent to 10 percent similar to changes from 10 percent to 5 percent, and accordingly advocated use of percent change in the poverty rate as the dependent variable. Using this dependent variable, Thornton, et al.'s dummy variable failed to be statistically significant for any demographic group regardless which of the two poverty definitions was employed. Hirsch

---

[33]Ibid., 393 and 394.

[34]Barry T. Hirsch, "Poverty and Economic Growth: Has Trickle Down Petered Out?" Economic Inquiry, 18 (January, 1980), 152.

concluded that trickle down was not significantly weaker in the post-1963 period.

In their reply to Hirsch, Thornton, et al.[35] first defended their use of the absolute change in the poverty rate as the appropriate dependent variable, given that they sought to prove Anderson's specific formulation of the trickle down hypothesis. Next, they very cleverly illustrated that the Hirsch result inadvertently implied a gloomier verdict for the anti-poverty effectiveness of growth than did their own findings. This twist came because as the poverty rate diminishes, Hirsch's improvements in poverty, a steady percent change in the poverty rate, when translated into numbers of people, becomes a smaller and smaller number. To illustrate, Thornton, et al. supposed that real per capita GNP increased at an average 2.93 percent rate. Hirsch's model predicted that would take sixteen years to halve the number of poor families from the 1974 level. Their own model implied eleven years.

A modern contribution to this discussion that was generally not in the technical mode was made by Charles Murray (1982). Its nontechnical style was more similar

---

[35]Richard R. Thornton, et al., "Poverty and Economic Growth: Trickle Down Has Petered Out," Economic Inquiry, 18 (January, 1980), 159-63.

to that of Galbraith and Harrington, although he did undertake some statistical analysis and did report the results of simple regression analysis. He regressed the first difference of the poverty rate on the first difference in real GNP per household over the period 1950 to 1980, found a close correlation, and concluded that "the effects of economic growth did indeed trickle down to the lowest economic levels of the society." Although this was the only regression he reported, he did further claim that "once the effects of GNP are taken into account, increases in social welfare spending do not account for reductions in poverty during the last three decades."[36] He offered no evidence for this contention.

Gottschalk and Danziger (henceforth, G&D) made three contributions to the technical literature.[37] In a 1983 paper they criticized the previous studies for their failure to provide a conceptual framework that linked the macroeconomic conditions and income transfers to

[36]Charles A. Murray, "The Two Wars Against Poverty," The Public Interest, 69 (Fall, 1982), 3-16.

[37]Peter Gottschalk and Sheldon Danziger, "Changes in Poverty, 1967-1982: Methodological Issues and Evidence," Discussion Paper No. 737-83, Institute for Research on Poverty (1983); "A Framework for Evaluating the Effects of Economic Growth and Transfers on Poverty," American Economic Review, 75 (March, 1985); "Do Rising Tides Lift All Boats? The Impact of Secular and Cyclical Changes on Poverty," American Economic Review, 76, (May, 1986).

reductions in poverty. That is, G&D charged that without an explicit theoretical foundation, there was little to guide the previous authors in their choices of variables or functional form. To illustrate the difficulty G&D estimated several equations making seemingly innocuous substitutions of proxies for the variables. The substitutions (for example, of the log of real median family income for real GNP per capita as the growth variable) had large impacts on the signs, magnitudes, and significance levels of the coefficients.

G&D attributed the lack of coefficient stability to the high collinearity among the independent variables. Consequently, G&D concluded that these time-series regressions provide little understanding of the relationship between economic growth, increases in transfers, and reductions in poverty.

A second contribution of G&D was their development of a new framework which was first presented in the 1983 paper, which reappeared with only slight refinements in a 1985 publication and which was the basis for the empirical results of a 1986 paper. Their conceptualization was to view poverty as cumulative density of income up to the "official" poverty line, where income consists of the sum of market and transfer incomes. However, since the "official" poverty line varied by family size, for convenience they utilized the distribution of households' income-to-needs ratio, with the poverty cutoff defined as an income-to-needs ratio less than one. Viewed this way, the change in poverty depends on the changes in the means and dispersions of each income source, their covariance and the displacement factor of their assumed distributions. G&D derived an equation which specifically dissected changes in poverty into changes in those moments.

Their empirical exercises led them to the following conclusion:

> During the 1967-79 period, changes in transfers were about as important as increases in market incomes for all persons. Transfers were less important for non-aged men, and very important for the elderly. Since 1979, the decline in market incomes has increased poverty, and the antipoverty effect of transfers growth has declined. Rising inequality increased poverty for all persons and for each group analyzed during the period of growth as well as during the recent recessionary period.[38]

In their 1986 paper G&D discussed separately three factors limiting the anti-poverty effectiveness of economic growth. They first held that an increasing proportion of the poor households were headed by individuals who, given their perceptions of "today's

_____

[38]Gottschalk and Danziger, (1985), 160.

social norms," would not be expected to work - namely, the elderly, students, the disabled, and women with a child under the age of six. Next, they statistically supported Anderson's thesis that the non-linear relationship between growth and poverty reduction contributed significantly to the diminished impact of growth on poverty. Finally, G&D demonstrated that increased inequality was a main factor serving to increase poverty during recoveries as well as recessions since 1969. However, they reported that the cause of the increased inequality was not understood.

VI: Critique of the Statistical Studies

As indicated in the preceding review of the literature, the modern discussion of the anti-poverty effectiveness of economic growth began with Galbraith's descriptions of "case" and "insular" poverties and Harrington's depiction of the changing nature of economic growth. These early studies were reasoned explanations of why economic growth could not be counted upon to alleviate U.S. poverty and, again, they centered around descriptions and understandings of the characteristics of poverty and the characteristics of economic growth.

In contrast the studies which followed contained very little economic explanation. Anderson directed the effort towards the statistical modeling of the relationship between the two variables of economic growth and poverty rates. Thus the discussion turned towards considerations of functional form based on the mathematical tautology that the size and shape of the income distribution yields the change in the poverty rate. The premise was that if the relationship could be correctly modeled then, by extrapolation, the future anti-poverty effectiveness of economic growth could be anticipated.

This approach has the basic weakness that it is static in nature. It assumes that the factors which yielded the growth/poverty relationship in the past did not and will not change over time. Consequently even if one develops a model with a very good "fit," the extrapolated impact of growth on poverty may be incorrect if there is a change in the underlying nature of the poverty problem or variation in the characteristics of economic growth.

The efforts to model the relationship between economic growth and poverty culminated in the sophisticated exercise of Gottschalk and Danziger. They recognized that it is not simply the changes in mean income (the usual proxy for economic growth) that affect the poverty rate but also changes in the variance and skewness of the income distribution. Furthermore, incomes come in two main forms: through the market and via transfers. G&D precisely related changes in the poverty rate to changes in the various moments of both of these income sources.

This approach is very useful for looking back and observing the impacts on the poverty rate of changes in market inequality, mean market incomes, and mean transfer incomes. However, the model is not useful for anticipating the future anti-poverty effectiveness of economic growth and in fact the authors did not draw from their model implications on that score.

VII: A Suggested Alternative Approach

An avenue is needed by which to better understand and anticipate the anti-poverty effectiveness of economic growth. We would do well to return to the early approaches of Galbraith and Harrington. What they provided was economic theory to explain the anticipated failure of growth to remedy poverty. Galbraith emphasized the nature of the poverty problem and Harrington emphasized the changed nature of economic growth. Thus they provided consideration of the factors which impact the anti-poverty effectiveness of economic growth.

This is the approach adopted in this dissertation. That is, in order to anticipate the anti-poverty effectiveness of economic growth, we need an understanding of the factors which over time strengthen or weaken the link between the two phenomena.

I will examine the anti-poverty effectiveness of economic growth in the light of two significant factors which impact the reliability of growth at combating poverty. It is not suggested that these are the only two factors which are important. However the two factors considered are critical to an understanding of the effectiveness of economic growth at reducing poverty, the change over time in that effectiveness, and the expected anti-poverty impact of economic growth.

CHAPTER 2:

DIVORCE AND THE POVERTY OF WOMEN

I: Introduction

The debate reviewed in Chapter 1 indicated that there has been disagreement concerning the extent to which economic growth may be depended upon to alleviate official poverty. As previously illustrated, the prior studies sought to establish the statistical relationship between economic growth and poverty reduction. However, the successful modeling of the historic pattern of the income and poverty relationship leaves a critical issue unresolved. Namely, what factors determine the strength of that relationship? What makes aggregate economic growth more or less effective at reducing poverty?

One factor which affects the anti-poverty effectiveness of growth is the phenomenon of divorce. As will be shown below divorce in the United States generally increased throughout the 1960s and 1970s and has continued at historically high levels through the early 1980s. This greater rate of divorce has diminished the effectiveness of economic growth at reducing aggregate poverty by expanding the group that has traditionally suffered higher rates of poverty: households that are headed by women.

44

This chapter first reviews the economic consequences of divorce for women and the extent of divorce in recent years. These considerations, addressed in Sections II and III, suggest a significant impact of divorce on the anti-poverty effectiveness of economic growth. The second principal focus of the chapter is upon the extent of poverty among women. The official poverty data concerning women will be closely analyzed in Sections IV through VI. Section VII summarizes the chapter.

II: The Economic Impact of Divorce on Women: Three Recent Studies

In a longitudinal study conducted by the Institute for Survey Research of the University of Michigan, the economic status of approximately 2400 women was observed over the seven year period 1968 through 1974.[1] The study related changes in economic status to changes in marital status. Two measures of economic status were employed. They were real income and the real "income-to-needs" ratio, where "needs" for every size of family were equated to 1.25 times the official poverty threshold for that family size.

---

[1] Saul Hoffman and John Holmes, "Husbands, Wives, and Divorce," in Five Thousand American Families – Patterns of Economic Progress, ed. by Greg J. Duncan and James N. Morgan (Ann Arbor, Michigan: Institute For Social Research, The University of Michigan, 1976).

All of the women in the sample were married in 1968;
by 1974 5.6 percent of the women were divorced or
separated from their husbands. Over the study period the
real mean income of women who were divorced or separated
dropped 29.3 percent, and the mean ratio of their real
income to their needs declined 6.7 percent. For the
group who remained married throughout the period the
percentage change in average real income was a positive
21.7 percent, and the percentage change in the real
income-to-needs ratio was a positive 20.8 percent.
Nearly 60 percent of the women who were divorced,
separated, or widowed experienced a decline in their real
income-to-needs ratio compared to 35 percent of the women
who remained married. Almost 15 percent of the divorced,
separated, or widowed group had declines of economic
status of more than 50 percent compared to only 4
percent of the always married women.[2] When additional
variables of race, age, education, city size, and region
were accounted for, the basic finding remained that
"changes in economic status were related to changes in
marital status. Women who remained married throughout

---

[2]Ibid., 31-32.

the seven-year period fared far better than did those who
were divorced, separated or widowed in 1974."[3]

A second study to examine the economic consequences
of divorce was based on in-depth interviews with a
randomly selected group of recently divorced men and
women in the Los Angeles area in 1978.[4] In her study
Lenore Weitzman employed as a measure of standard of
living the income-to-needs ratio of the previous study.
She reported that in the year following a divorce men
experienced a 42 percent improvement in their standard of
living while women experienced a 73 percent loss. The
data suggested to Weitzman "that divorce is a financial
catastrophe for most women: in just one year they
experience a dramatic decline in income and a calamitous
drop in their standard of living."[5]

Finally, a survey of the evidence of the economic
consequences on women of marriage dissolution was
presented by the New Jersey Supreme Court Task Force on

[3]Ibid., 44.

[4]Lenore J. Weitzman, "The Economics of Divorce:
Social and Economic Consequences of Property, Alimony and
Child Support Awards," UCLA Law Review, vol. 28 (August,
1981), 1181-1268.

[5]Ibid., 1252.

Women in the Courts.[6] The Task Force noted a wide array of statistics which point to a detrimental economic impact of divorce on women. Included were the higher poverty rates of families maintained by women when compared to all other families (see Table 2.1 below), and the widely recognized inequity between the wages of full-time year-round women and men workers which in 1982 was 62 cents for women for every one dollar earned by men. Further evidence included the discrepancy in 1982 of 3.76 billion dollars between child support payments that were due and those payments that were received, and the over representation of widowed, divorced, and single women among the elderly poor.[7] Based on these and other national data the Task Force concluded that

> it is evident that many, and perhaps most, women suffer disproportionate hardship as a consequence of separation and divorce. Employment discrimination, grossly insufficient child care facilities, inflation, inadequate child spousal support awards and widespread defaults in payment of child and spousal support obligations conjoin to drive single

---

[6]New Jersey Supreme Court Task Force on Women in the Courts, "The First Year Report of the New Jersey Supreme Court Task Force on Women in the Courts – June 1984," Women's Rights Law Reporter, vol. 9, no. 2 (Spring, 1986).

[7]Ibid., 155-156.

women and their children below poverty levels
in alarming numbers.[8]

Although none of these studies directly demonstrated
the extent to which divorce precipitates official
impoverishment, the evidence does support the hypothesis
that divorce introduces many women and their dependent
children to official poverty status. The following
section will develop rough but illustrative indications
of the number of instances that divorce has placed some
individual woman or dependent child into the
economically vulnerable demographic groups of households
headed by women.

III: Divorce and the Decline into Poverty

It is readily apparent from the official poverty
counts that in any given year families that are headed by
women are more likely to be poor than are all other
families. Similarly, female unrelated individuals are
more often poor than are male unrelated individuals. The
poverty rates of female-headed families, all other
families, and female and male unrelated individuals are

---

[8]Ibid., 165. The implication that divorce is
economically harmful to women based on these types of
cross-sectional evidence has been common among the
scholars of divorce and the impoverishment of women. See
for example Diana Pearce, "The Feminization of Poverty:
Women, Work, and Welfare," Urban and Social Change
Review, (February, 1978).

presented in Table 2.1 and Figure 2.1. The net declines in the poverty rates from 1959 to 1985 are readily apparent. While the net decline in the poverty rate of each of these demographic groups served to diminish the total number of poor people within the nation, divorce acted as an opposing force serving to increase both the absolute number of poor and the aggregate poverty rate. That is, since divorce increases the number of female-headed families and female unrelated individuals, it increases the proportion of the total population that lives in households headed by women and which faces a greater vulnerability to poverty.

A simple illustration of the magnitude of the potential impact of divorce will be offered. This will be obtained by estimating the number of occurrences of a woman or of a child coming to live either in a female-headed family or as a female unrelated individual and thereby entering the group of individuals which is particularly vulnerable to official impoverishment. The U.S. Department of Health and Human Services provides estimates of various statistics related to divorce in the United States. Column 1 of Table 2.2 and the accompanying Figure 2.2 indicate their estimate of the number of divorces each year from 1959 through 1983. Since each divorce yields one unmarried woman this series

Table 2.1:   Poverty   rates of   female-headed families, all other families, and unrelated individuals by sex, 1959-1985

Year	Female-headed families	All other families	Female unrelated individuals	Male unrelated individuals
1959	42.6	15.8	52.1	36.8
1960	42.4	15.4	50.9	36.1
1961	42.1	15.4	52.4	36.0
1962	42.9	14.3	51.0	36.5
1963	40.4	13.1	50.0	34.8
1964	36.4	12.5	49.3	32.0
1965	38.4	11.1	46.2	28.9
1966	33.1	9.3	43.5	29.3
1967	33.3	8.7	44.7	26.9
1968	32.3	7.3	39.2	25.4
1969	32.6	6.9	38.7	26.2
1970	32.5	7.2	38.4	24.0
1971	33.9	6.8	36.6	23.9
1972	32.7	6.1	34.3	21.1
1973	32.2	5.5	29.7	19.8
1974	32.1	5.4	27.3	19.5
1975	32.5	6.2	28.9	19.9
1976	33.0	5.6	28.7	19.7
1977	31.7	5.5	26.1	18.0
1978	31.4	5.3	26.0	17.1
1979	30.4	5.5	26.0	16.9
1980	32.7	6.3	27.4	17.4
1981	34.6	7.0	27.7	18.1
1982	36.3	7.9	26.6	18.8
1983	36.0	7.8	25.6	20.1
1984	34.5	7.2	24.4	18.7
1985	34.0	7.0	24.8	17.4

Source: Current Population Reports P-60 Series, various years.

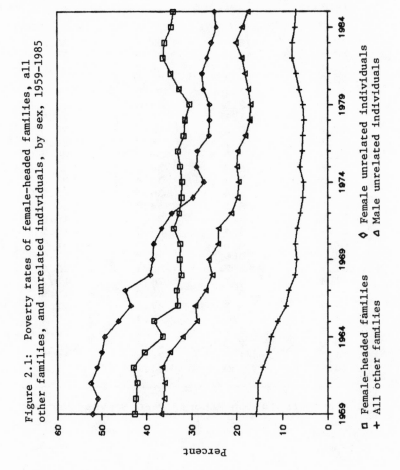

Figure 2.1: Poverty rates of female-headed families, all other families, and unrelated individuals, by sex, 1959-1985

□ Female-headed families   ◇ Female unrelated individuals
+ All other families   △ Male unrelated individuals

Source: Table 2.1

Table 2.2:   Estimated   number of instances that a woman or child came to live in a female-headed household following a divorce, all estimates in thousands

Year	(1) Number of divorces	(2) Estimated number of children involved in divorce	(3)* Estimated number of children to live in female-headed families after divorce	(4)** Estimated number of individuals to live in female-headed households after divorce
1959	395	468	397.8	792.8
1960	393	463	393.6	786.6
1961	414	516	438.6	852.6
1962	413	532	452.2	865.2
1963	428	562	477.7	905.7
1964	450	613	521.1	971.7
1965	479	630	535.5	1014.5
1966	499	669	568.7	1067.7
1967	523	701	595.9	1118.9
1968	584	784	666.4	1250.4
1969	639	840	714.0	1353.0
1970	708	870	739.5	1447.5
1971	773	946	804.1	1577.1
1972	845	1021	867.9	1712.9
1973	915	1079	917.2	1832.2
1974	977	1099	934.2	1911.2
1975	1036	1123	954.6	1990.6
1976	1083	1117	949.5	2032.5
1977	1091	1095	930.8	2021.8
1978	1130	1147	975.0	2105.0
1979	1181	1181	1003.9	2184.9
1980	1189	1174	997.9	2186.9
1981	1213	1180	1003.0	2216.0
1982	1170	1108	941.8	2111.8
1983	1158	1091	927.4	2085.4

*(3) = (2) × (0.85)
**(4) = (1) + (3)

Sources: U.S. Department of Health and Human Services, Vital Statistics of the United States 1982, Vol. III: Marriage and Divorce (Washington, D.C.:   U.S. Government Printing Office), Tables 2-1 and 2-11; and The Statistical Abstract 1987, 80.

Figure 2.2: Number of divorces, 1959–1983

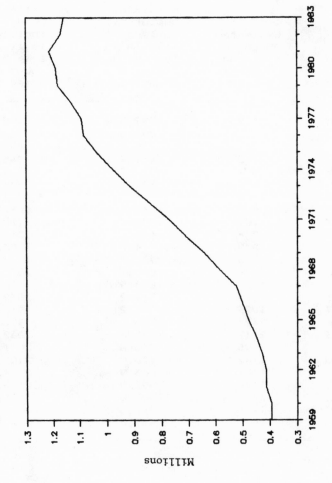

Source: Table 2.2, Column 1

also serves as an estimate of the number of times that a woman became a head of a new family unit or became a female unrelated individual. While this method overstates the number of women affected due to repeated counting associated with repeated divorces, it does provide a reflection of the number of times that some individual became a member of the population of female-headed households and female unrelated individuals.

Column 2 lists the estimates of the annual total number of children under the age of 18 years whose parents divorced in that year. There is a difficulty in estimating the number of these children who subsequently lived with their mothers in a female-headed family. The difficulty stems from the lack of a nationwide study of custody awards. However after reviewing the available evidence, Weitzman concluded that over the past century mothers have been awarded custody of the children in approximately 85 percent of all divorce cases.[9] This percentage will be used to estimate the number of instances that a child lived with his or her mother subsequent to a divorce. Two formidable problems are evident when employing Weitzman's percentage for this

---

[9]Lenore J. Weitzman, The Divorce Revolution (New York: The Free Press, 1985), 222.

purpose. It ignores both a possible bias caused by a correlation between the likelihood of maternal custody awards and the number of dependents, and the possibility that in recent years the percentage has significantly deviated from the average over the last century. However the present task is to obtain a general indication of the number of times that a child came to live in female-headed families as a consequence of divorce. For this illustrative purpose the Weitzman estimate is held to suffice.

The multiplication of the number of children involved in divorce times 85 percent provides a rough estimate of the number of times that a child came to live in female-headed families following the divorce of his or her parents. This estimate appears in Column 3. The estimate of the number instances that a woman or a child entered a female-headed household is the sum of Columns 1 and 3 and is provided in Column 4. This series represents the number of instances that an individual's chance of being impoverished increased significantly due to a divorce. This figure has generally grown over the time period from less than 800,000 per year to over 2 million per year. The trend is represented in Figure 2.3.

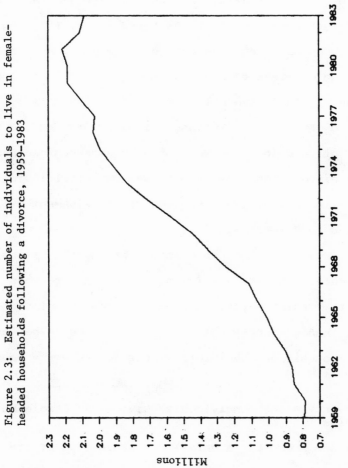

Figure 2.3: Estimated number of individuals to live in female-headed households following a divorce, 1959-1983

Source: Table 2.2, Column 4

It is not suggested that all the newly formed female-headed families and new female unrelated individuals that do slip into poverty remain in poverty. Possible escape routes include remarriage and work outside the home. However, as noted above, it is agreed that divorce has precipitated a decline into poverty for increasing millions of American women and their dependent children. This exercise indicates the large and increased number of instances in which an individual's chances of becoming poor were greatly enhanced because of marital dissolution. A more formal empirical indication of the link between divorce and impoverishment will be presented in Chapter 5.

In sum, divorce increases the number among the entire population who are for a variety of reasons less likely to escape poverty through the rewards of economic growth. Hence higher rates of divorce are expected to render economic growth a less viable anti-poverty weapon.

IV: Poverty Among Individuals Living in Female-Headed Households

We now turn to a detailed examination of the data which represent the poverty of women in the United States. Poverty among women is commonly viewed from two demographic perspectives. They are, first, the proportion of the population, including children and unrelated females, who live in poor households that are headed by women and have no husband present. This group is referred to as "female-headed households," often denoted "FHH." The second demographic perspective is the proportion of the population of adult women that is poor, including poor wives. Data on both groups will be presented in order to get a broader picture of the impoverishment of women. I will begin with the latter demographic perspective of individuals living in households headed by women.

Estimates of the number of the poor individuals living in households with a female head have been provided annually by the Bureau of the Census. These figures are provided in Column 1 of Table 2.3 and in the accompanying Figure 2.4. The number of poor individuals in FHHs held relatively stable from 1959 through the early 1970s, but then generally increased through 1984.

Two national trends make the record of Column 1 difficult to access. They are the shift in the demographic composition of the population into female-headed households and the overall increase in the total U.S. population. Columns 2 through 5 and Figures 2.4 and 2.5 are offered to provide a wider perspective on the data. Column 2 (also depicted in Figure 2.4)

Table 2.3: Poverty among individuals living in female-headed households, 1959-1984

	(1) Poor living in FHHs*	(2) Population living in FHHs*	(3) Population in FHHs as percentage of U.S. population	(4) Poverty rate of FHHs	(5) Poor in FHHs as percentage of U.S. population
1959	10.39	20.70	11.7	50.2	5.8
1960	10.67	21.54	11.9	49.5	5.9
1961	10.80	21.81	11.9	49.5	5.9
1962	11.23	22.24	11.9	50.5	6.0
1963	11.10	22.93	12.1	48.4	5.9
1964	10.97	23.90	12.5	45.9	5.7
1965	11.06	24.04	12.4	46.0	5.7
1966	10.25	25.00	12.7	41.0	5.2
1967	10.59	26.09	13.1	40.6	5.3
1968	10.36	26.64	13.3	38.9	5.2
1969	10.41	27.12	13.4	38.4	5.1
1970	11.15	29.20	14.2	38.2	5.4
1971	11.41	30.02	14.5	38.0	5.5
1972	11.59	31.40	15.0	36.9	5.5
1973	11.36	32.54	15.4	34.9	5.4
1974	11.47	34.13	16.0	33.6	5.4
1975	12.27	35.46	16.4	34.6	5.7
1976	12.59	36.59	16.8	34.4	5.8
1977	12.62	38.49	17.5	32.8	5.7
1978	12.88	39.88	17.9	32.3	5.9
1979	13.50	42.20	18.7	32.0	6.0
1980	14.65	43.34	19.0	33.8	6.4
1981	15.74	44.71	19.4	35.2	6.8
1982	16.34	45.13	19.4	36.2	7.0
1983	16.71	46.95	20.0	35.6	7.1
1984	16.44	48.35	20.4	34.0	7.1

*=in millions.

Source: Bureau of the Census, Current Population Reports P-60 Series, various years, and The Statistical Abstract of the United States 1986.

61

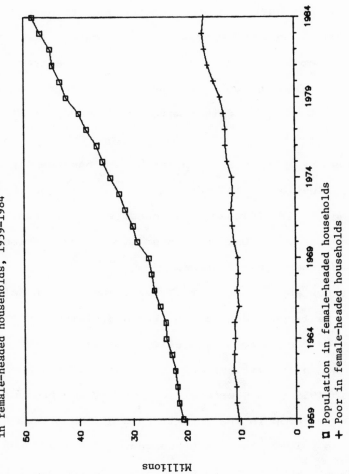

Figure 2.4: Poor in female-headed households and population in female-headed households, 1959–1984

□ Population in female-headed households
+ Poor in female-headed households

Source: Table 2.3, Columns 1 and 2

indicates the total number of individuals living in FHHs, and Column 3 represents this total group as a percentage of the U.S. population. As evidenced, the shift of the population into FHHs has occurred throughout the period.

Column 4 registers the poverty rate for this demographic group and shows that the pattern was strongly downward through 1979 when it then began to rise again. This trend combined with the demographic trend resulted in the record of Column 5, the FHH poor as a percentage of the U.S. population. There was little annual fluctuation in this ratio and virtually no change over time. It reached its lowest values in the late 1960s and early 1970s, and over the time period it registered a small net increase.

It is now apparent that this small increase in Column 5 hides the larger changes in the underlying variables which yield the ratio. The slight increase in the poor in FHHs as a percentage of the population from 5.9 percent in 1959 to 6.9 percent in 1984 was the product of a substantial drop in the poverty rate of FHHs from 50.2 percent in 1959 to 34.0 percent in 1984 and a significant increase in the proportion of the population that lived in FHHs from 11.7 percent to 20.4 percent. These three series are presented in Figure 2.5.

63

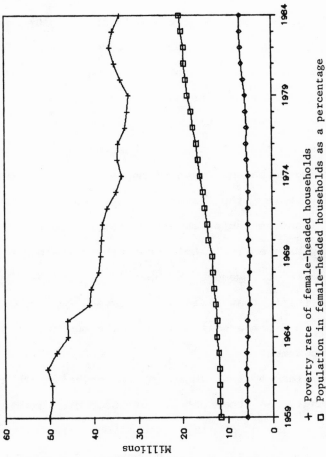
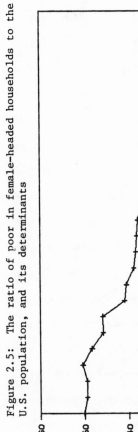

Figure 2.5: The ratio of poor in female-headed households to the U.S. population, and its determinants

+ Poverty rate of female-headed households
□ Population in female-headed households as a percentage of U.S. population
◊ Poor in female-headed households as a percentage of U.S. population

Source: Table 2.3, Columns 3, 4, and 5

The analysis will now turn to an empirical indication of the relative strengths of these factors. To begin an important assumption must be made. In this analysis I will assume that the change in the poverty rate is independent of the demographic shift. Of course this assumption ignores the possible causal links between the demographic composition of the population and the poverty rate of female-headed households. The most obvious link between the demographic factor and the poverty rate is the potential labor supply impact. That is, as more women become heads of households, they might increasingly enter the labor market, push down their wages and increase their poverty rates. However, this familiar logical analysis holds restricted the number of jobs available to women. What if, instead, the demographic shift that yielded more women employees was accompanied by a comparable growth in the number of jobs available to women?

It is clear that changes in the poverty rate also depend strongly on the degree of economic growth. A consistent movement of the population into FHHs may witness falling, steady, or rising poverty rates for FHHs depending on the performance of the economy in creating jobs for women. Actual historic evidence allows the assumption that poverty rates critically reflect economic growth and are independent of the demographic composition of the nation. The Pearson correlation coefficient between the poverty rate of FHHs and the FHH population as a percentage of the U.S. population is -0.83, a strong correlation but of the opposite sign predicted by the theory. In the absence of a feasible theory explaining a negative causal relationship between the two variables, it will be assumed that the impact of economic growth on the poverty rate has greatly dominated the labor supply effect leaving the poverty rate statistically independent of the demographic composition of the population.

With this assumption I can proceed with the descriptive analysis of the relative impacts of poverty rate changes and demographic changes on the poor living in FHHs as a percentage of the total U.S. population. In 1959 11.7 percent of the nation's population lived in FHHs (Table 2.3, Column 3) and 5.89 percent lived in poor female-headed households (Table 2.3, Column 5). If the 1959 demographic composition had been maintained, given the lower poverty rate of FHHs in 1984 (Table 2.3, Column 4), the FHH poor as a percentage of the U.S. population would have declined to 3.98 percent over the period. The actual 1984 ratio was 7.09. Hence the actual change from 5.89 percent in 1959 to 7.09 percent in 1984 is the sum

of the 1.91 percent reduction caused by the reduced
poverty rate (3.98 minus 5.89) and the remaining 3.11
percent increase (7.09 minus 3.98) resulting from the
demographic shift.   This decomposition of the net change
over the time period is presented in Table 2.4 (at the
bottom).

The separate impacts in each year are provided in
the same Table and in Figure 2.6.   In Figure 2.6 the
hatched line illustrates the impact of changing
demographics. In most years there was an increase in the
FHH population as a percentage of the U.S. population.
This served to increase (or cause a positive change in)
the poor living in FHHs as a percentage of the aggregate
population. In Figure 2.6 this is reflected by the
positive values associated with the impact of the
demographic factor.

The solid line reflects the impact of changes in the
poverty rate.   Years in which the poverty rate declined
and acted to reduce the poor in FHHs as a percentage of
the U.S. population are associated with negative values
in Figure 2.6. Years in which the poverty rate increased
and acted to increase the poor in FHHs as a percentage of
the U.S. population are indicated by positive values.

In this manner Figure 2.6 illustrates that in
virtually all years the demographic factor acted to

Table   2.4:   The poor   living in   FHHs as a percentage of the U.S.
population, 1959-1984

	(1)	(2)	(3)	(4)
Year	$\left[\dfrac{\text{Poor in FHHs}}{\text{U.S. population}}\right]$	Change in $\left[\dfrac{\text{Poor in FHHs}}{\text{U.S. population}}\right]$	Change attributed to change in poverty rate	Change attributed to change in demographic mix
1959	5.89	–	–	–
1960	5.95	0.06	-0.08	0.14
1961	5.96	0.01	0.00	0.01
1962	6.09	0.13	0.12	0.01
1963	5.92	-0.17	-0.25	0.08
1964	5.77	-0.15	-0.31	0.16
1965	5.77	0.00	0.01	-0.01
1966	5.28	-0.49	-0.63	0.14
1967	5.40	0.12	-0.05	0.17
1968	5.25	-0.15	-0.23	0.08
1969	5.24	-0.01	-0.07	0.06
1970	5.49	0.25	-0.30	0.28
1971	5.57	0.08	-0.03	0.11
1972	5.64	0.07	-0.16	0.23
1973	5.45	-0.20	-0.31	0.11
1974	5.46	0.01	-0.20	0.21
1975	5.84	0.38	0.16	0.22
1976	5.96	0.12	-0.03	0.15
1977	5.90	-0.06	-0.28	0.22
1978	5.97	0.07	-0.09	0.16
1979	6.09	0.12	-0.06	0.18
1980	6.48	0.39	0.34	0.05
1981	6.92	0.44	0.27	0.17
1982	7.12	0.20	0.20	0.00
1983	7.23	0.11	-0.12	0.23
1984	7.09	-0.14	-0.33	0.19
Net change from 1959-1984		1.20	-1.91	3.11

Source: Derived from Bureau of the Census P-60 Series, No. 152.

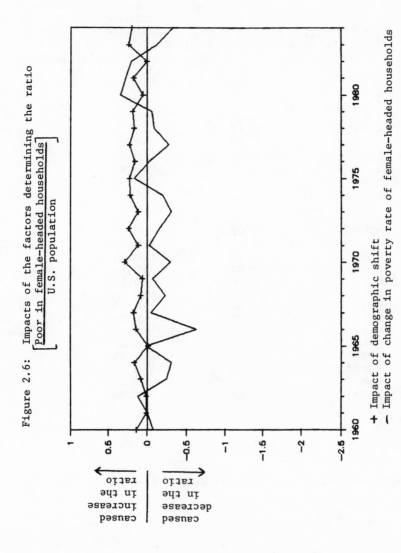

Figure 2.6: Impacts of the factors determining the ratio
$$\left[\frac{\text{Poor in female-headed households}}{\text{U.S. population}}\right]$$

+ Impact of demographic shift
– Impact of change in poverty rate of female-headed households

Source: Table 2.4, Columns 3 and 4

enhance the ratio of the poor in FHHs to the entire population. Effects of changes in the poverty rate were irregular in comparison. Generally through the early 1970s declines in the poverty rate worked counter to the demographic impacts, but in 1975 and again in the early 1980s increases in the poverty rate worked with the demographic changes to increase the ratio of the poor in FHHs to the total population.

V: A Comparison of Poverty Among Female-Headed Households to Poverty Among "Other-Headed Households"

For comparison, and in anticipation of the discussion of the "feminization of poverty" to follow in Chapter 3, analogous descriptive analyses will be offered for the remainder of the nation's households, the officially designated "all other" households. This group includes first all households other than those headed by women with no husband present, and in addition, male unrelated individuals. It will be denoted "OHH" indicating "other-headed households." Until the early 1980s this demographic group was designated as having a "male head" reflecting the view that if a husband was present, he was the family head. While this chauvinism has been removed from the official statistics, a problem of a similar ilk remains when these data are used to reflect the economic performances of women and men, a methodology that will be employed shortly. That is, I will relate the FHH poverty data to the economic performance of women and the OHH poverty data to the economic performance of men. The difficulty is readily apparent: the progress against the poverty of "other-headed households" reflects the market accomplishments of women (wives) as well as men (husbands). The emergence of an "other-headed household" from poverty may reflect the employment or enhanced wages of the wife and to attribute this change in poverty status to the male is incorrect.

The use of OHH poverty data as an indicator of the economic performance of men will be defended on two grounds. First, the economic successes and failures of men do dramatically impact the poverty status of OHHs. As will be discussed in detail in Chapter 4, men typically receive higher earnings than women. Consequently men's incomes impact more critically on the economic welfare of the other-headed household.

Second, there are no alternative poverty data available. By definition the official poverty measure varies with family size. Either the entire household is in poverty or it is not in poverty and the designation depends on the household's gross income. Thus there is no way to examine solely the poverty of husbands and ignore the financial contributions of the wives. Even if one sought to subtract the wives' incomes and evaluate the households' poverty status on the basis of the husbands' incomes alone, it would be problematic. For example, in the absence of the wives' incomes, husbands may well work harder, work overtime, or carry more than one job.

As with FHHs, the poverty rate of OHHs is assumed to be independent of the demographic mix. The data for OHHs are presented in Table 2.5 and Figure 2.7. In the Figure the hatched line again represents the impact of the demographic shift and the solid line reflects the impact of the changing poverty rates. Contrasts between the records of FHHs and OHHs are apparent.

The first striking contrast is that over the time period while there was a slight increase in the FHH poor as a percentage of the U.S. population (5.8 to 6.9 percent) there was a sharp decline from 16.50 percent to 7.36 percent for OHH as a percent of the U.S. population. See Tables 2.4 and 2.5, Column 1.

A second contrast is the relative impact of the demographic shift. Because the OHH population was much larger than the FHH population, the demographic shift (of roughly 48 million individuals) had a relatively smaller impact and, of course, worked in the opposite direction.

Table   2.5:   The poor living in OHHs as a percentage of the U.S. population, 1959-1984

	(1)	(2)	(3)	(4)
Year	$\left[\dfrac{\text{Poor in OHHs}}{\text{U.S. population}}\right]$	Change in $\left[\dfrac{\text{Poor in OHHs}}{\text{U.S. population}}\right]$	Change attributed to change in poverty rate	Change attributed to change in demographic mix
1959	16.50	-	-	-
1960	16.28	-0.22	-0.18	-0.04
1961	15.92	-0.36	-0.35	-0.01
1962	14.86	-1.06	-1.06	-0.00
1963	13.52	-1.34	-1.32	-0.02
1964	13.20	-0.32	-0.26	-0.06
1965	11.54	-1.66	-1.66	0.00
1966	9.41	-2.13	-2.10	-0.03
1967	8.76	-0.65	-0.61	-0.04
1968	7.61	-1.15	-1.13	-0.02
1969	6.91	-0.70	-0.69	-0.01
1970	7.02	0.11	0.17	-0.06
1971	6.91	-0.11	-0.09	-0.02
1972	6.27	-0.64	-0.60	-0.04
1973	5.57	-0.70	-0.68	-0.02
1974	5.95	0.37	0.42	-0.05
1975	6.48	0.53	0.59	-0.06
1976	5.97	-0.61	-0.58	-0.03
1977	5.66	-0.21	-0.17	-0.04
1978	5.38	-0.36	-0.25	-0.11
1979	5.67	0.29	0.33	-0.04
1980	6.47	0.80	0.80	-0.01
1981	7.07	0.60	0.65	-0.05
1982	7.87	0.80	0.80	-0.00
1983	8.04	0.18	0.24	-0.05
1984	7.36	-0.69	-0.64	-0.05
Net change from 1959-1984		-9.14	-8.28	-0.86

Source: Derived from Bureau of the Census P-60 Series, No. 152.

73

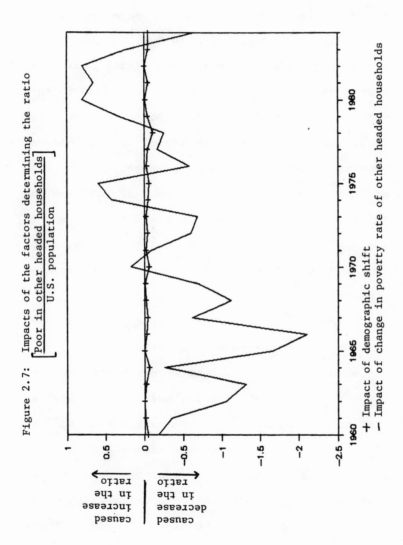

Figure 2.7: Impacts of the factors determining the ratio

$$\left[\frac{\text{Poor in other headed households}}{\text{U.S. population}}\right]$$

+ Impact of demographic shift
− Impact of change in poverty rate of other headed households

Source: Table 2.5, Columns 3 and 4

That is, over the time period the shift of the population into FHHs served to add 3.11 percent to the FHH poor as a percentage of the population (Table 2.4, Column 4), yet the shift reduced the OHH poor as a percentage of the population by only 0.86 percent (Table 2.5, Column 4).

Since the total change is the sum of the impact of the demographic shift and the impact of changes in the poverty rate, this small impact for OHHs of the demographic factor implies that the impact of the changes in the poverty rate was relatively large. Figure 2.7 illustrates this point well. The impact of changes in the poverty rate are clearly seen to dominate the impact of the demographic shift. Generally in the first part of the period the poverty rate declined and thereby worked to reduce the ratio of the poor in OHHs to the U.S. population. Increasingly in the later years, higher poverty rates worked to increase this ratio.

A third more subtle contrast between the records of FHHs and OHHs is important in the light of the analysis that will follow in Chapter 3. In comparing Figures 2.6 and 2.7 (which are graphed to the same scale), it is apparent that in determining the ratio of the poor to the population as a whole, changes in the poverty rates were a stronger factor for OHHs than they were for FHHs. This is because the changes in the poverty rates of the OHHs were proportionately larger than the changes experienced by FHHs. That is, the poverty rate of OHHs declined from 18.7 percent in 1959 to its lowest value in 1978 of 6.6 percent. This represented a 65 percent drop from the initial value. The decline for FHHs from 50.2 percent in 1959 to its lowest value of 32.0 percent in 1979 represented a drop of only 36 percent from its initial value. Furthermore, the percentage increases in the poverty rate in the 1970s and early 1980s for OHH exceeded the percentage setbacks for FHHs.

Three questions emerge from these statistics which describe the poverty of FHHs and OHHs. First, why are FHH poverty rates higher than OHH poverty rates? Second, compared to the poverty rates of OHHs, why did the poverty rates among FHHs register smaller percentage improvements from 1959 through the late 1970s? Third, compared to the poverty rates of OHHs, why did the poverty rates among FHHs increase by smaller percentage amounts in the late 1970s and early 1980s? These questions will emerge again in the discussion of the "feminization of poverty" in the following chapter. The answers to the questions will be developed in Chapters 4 and 5 and will center around the pattern of sex segregation in the labor market and the sectoral composition of economic growth.

VI: Poor Adults

The second demographic perspective on the poverty of women is to view directly the adult female population. An immediate problem arises when counts of poor adult women are sought. The difficulty is that no consistent published series is available for poor adult females that covers the entire period since 1959. The Bureau of the Census began only in 1969 to provide estimates of the absolute number of poor women, regardless of family status. For the present analysis it has been possible to estimate the simple count of the number of poor women for 1959 through 1973 from an alternative Census source. (See Appendix 1 for an explanation of the estimation process.) Those estimates are provided in Column 1 of Table 2.6. Column 3 reports the Census estimates for 1969 through 1984. Figure 2.8 presents both of these data series. For comparison the analogously derived data for men are also presented in Table 2.6 Columns 5 and 7 and in Figure 2.8.

As in the case of female-headed households, the growth in the nation's population creates a difficulty in perceiving the degree of improvement associated with this record. Hence Columns 2 and 4 indicate that as a percentage of the U.S. population, the group of poor adult women declined through the mid 1970s and increased

Table 2.6: The number of poor adults (in millions), and poor adults as a percentage of the U.S. population, by sex, 1959-1984

	Poor adult women, author's estimate	Previous column as percentage of U.S. population	Poor adult women, Census estimate	Previous column as percentage of U.S. population	Poor adult men, author's estimate	Previous column as percentage of U.S. population	Poor adult men, author's estimate	Previous column as precentage of U.S. population
1959	11.5	6.5	*na	na	8.0	4.5	na	na
1960	11.5	6.3	na	na	7.8	4.3	na	na
1961	11.7	6.4	na	na	8.0	4.4	na	na
1962	11.3	6.1	na	na	7.6	4.1	na	na
1963	10.8	5.7	na	na	7.1	3.7	na	na
1964	10.7	5.6	na	na	6.8	3.5	na	na
1965	10.1	5.2	na	na	6.1	3.1	na	na
1966	9.1	4.6	na	na	5.4	2.7	na	na
1967	9.3	4.7	na	na	5.2	2.6	na	na
1968	8.3	4.2	na	na	4.6	2.3	na	na
1969	8.5	4.2	8.2	4.0	4.6	2.3	4.6	2.3
1970	8.8	4.3	8.5	4.2	4.7	2.3	4.7	2.3
1971	8.8	4.3	8.5	4.1	4.7	2.3	4.6	2.2
1972	8.5	4.0	8.1	3.9	4.3	2.1	4.3	2.0
1973	7.9	3.7	7.6	3.6	4.1	1.9	4.0	1.9
1974	8.2	3.9	7.8	3.6	4.4	2.0	4.2	2.0
1975	na	na	8.2	3.8	na	na	4.5	2.1
1976	na	na	8.3	3.8	na	na	4.4	2.0
1977	na	na	8.1	3.7	na	na	4.4	2.0
1978	na	na	8.2	3.7	na	na	4.3	1.9
1979	na	na	8.6	3.8	na	na	4.7	2.1
1980	na	na	10.0	4.4	na	na	5.5	2.4
1981	na	na	10.7	4.7	na	na	6.0	2.6
1982	na	na	11.3	4.9	na	na	6.7	2.9
1983	na	na	11.6	4.9	na	na	7.1	3.0
1984	na	na	10.9	4.9	na	na	6.7	2.8

*not available

Source: see Appendix

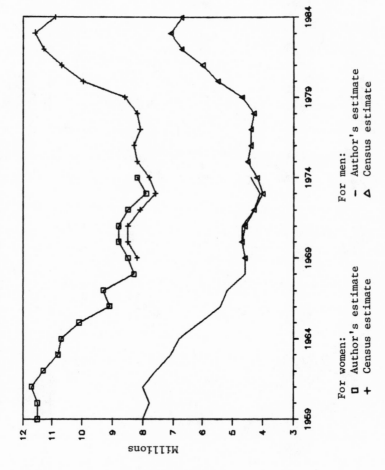

Figure 2.8: Poor adults, by sex, 1959-1984

For women:
  □ Author's estimate
  + Census estimate

For men:
  − Author's estimate
  △ Census estimate

Source: Table 2.6, Columns 1, 3, 5, and 7

in the early 1980s. This record is provided graphically in Figure 2.9. Again the analogous data for men are presented in Table 2.6 Columns 6 and 8 and in Figure 2.9.

Based on these observations of women, measured both by a head count and as a percentage of the U.S. population, the poverty of adult women first diminished markedly through the 1960s and into the 1970s but then generally increased through the mid 1980s. There was however a net improvement over the time period. As for poor men throughout the period their absolute number was consistently around four million less than that of poor women. Similar to the trend among women, the number of poor men fell through the early 1970s and then in the late 1970s began to rise again. As a percentage of the total population, poor men, as poor women, declined until the late 1970s and then increased.

As in the previous discussion of households there is a discrepancy between the performance of women and men. The decline in the ratio of poor adult women to the total population from its peak to its lowest value represented a 43 percent improvement, while this ratio for men improved by 58 percent. Also late in the period the men suffered greater percentage setbacks against poverty than did women.

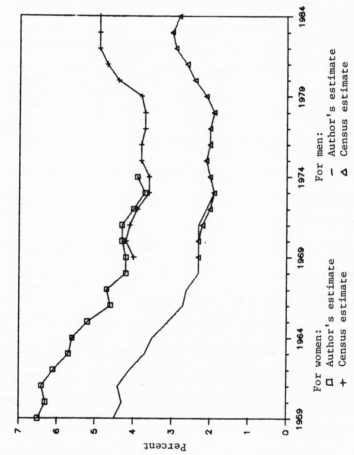

Figure 2.9: Poor adults as a percentage of U.S. population,
by sex, 1959-1984

For women:
  □ Author's estimate
  + Census estimate

For men:
  — Author's estimate
  △ Census estimate

Source: Table 2.6, Columns 2, 4, 6, and 8

While recognizing that these data are not reliable for all purposes, they are offered as another signal of the general trend indicated in the previous section. Both data sets raise the same issues: Why are women's poverty rates higher than men's and why did women's poverty rates initially improve by proportionately less but later rise by proportionately less than did men's poverty rates?

VII: Summary

The economic consequences of divorce for women and their dependent children are detrimental. The evidence suggests that divorce precipitates a decline into poverty for many women and the families that they lead. The dramatic increase in the incidence of divorce has expanded this segment of our total population that is particularly vulnerable to poverty and that is less likely to share the benefits of a healthy economy. Hence my interest in divorce is based on its potential to render economic growth a less viable anti-poverty weapon.

The official impoverishment of women was viewed from two demographic perspectives: households that are headed by women and the adult female population. While the number of poor individuals living in female-headed households increased from 1959 to 1984, there was a rough consistency in the number of poor in FHHs as a percentage of the entire population. This consistency resulted despite the significant reductions in the poverty rate for female-headed households. These reductions in the poverty rate were offset by the demographic shift of the population into female-headed households. The ratio of the poor in OHHs to the nation's population was approximately cut in half over the study period. This significant reduction was largely the consequence of improvements in the group's poverty rate.

I then turned to the adult female and male populations. For the two sexes I observed both the number of poor and the poor as a percentage of the aggregate population. By each measure both groups experienced similar patterns of decreases in the early part of the period and increases in the later years.

It was shown that from both demographic perspectives that women suffer greater poverty than men; that in the 1960s and early 1970s, relative to men, women enjoyed smaller percentage improvements in their poverty rates; and in the early 1980s, compared to men, women suffered smaller percentage setbacks in their poverty rates.

It will be demonstrated in Chapter 3 that these patterns of change lie behind the phenomenon of the "feminization of poverty." Explanations for the varied poverty records of men and women will be developed in Chapter 4 and will be based upon examinations of sex segregation in the labor market and the sectoral composition of economic growth. In Chapter 5 divorce will appear in an empirical model which will test and predict the anti-poverty impact of economic growth.

CHAPTER 3:

THE FEMINIZATION OF POVERTY

I: Introduction

The wide recognition of the shift of the incidence
of poverty into female-headed households was prompted by
the observation of Diana Pearce.[1] In reference to this
trend she contributed the phrase "feminization of
poverty." In her view poverty was "rapidly becoming a
female problem." Evidence that she offered in support of
her thesis included statistics suggesting that in 1976
almost two-thirds of the poor over 16 years of age were
women, that more than 70 percent of the elderly poor in
that year were female, that between 1950 and 1976 there
was a doubling of the number of poor female-headed
households, and that at the time of her writing almost
half of all poor families were headed by women. It was
implicitly posited that each of these measures of the
feminization of poverty had been growing over time. She
concluded that "[i]t is women who account for an

_____

[1]Diana Pearce, "The Feminization of Poverty: Women,
Work, and Welfare," Urban and Social Change Review, 11,
no. 1 (February 1978), 28-36.

increasingly large portion of the econo\
disadvantaged."[2]

Thus, in general, the feminization of poverty refers to the percentage of total poverty that is suffered by women. Consequently, the concept emerges as a relative measure of the poverty of women in the sense that it is determined by the poverty of women relative to the poverty of men.

Given the wide recognition of the phrase, it is perhaps surprising to note that the feminization of poverty, its causes, and its recent reversal have not received widespread scholarly attention and have remained primarily in the domain of sociologists. Also, a serious omission from previous discussions of the feminization of poverty is a critique of its usefulness as an indicator of the economic well-being of women. These are the issues addressed in this chapter and the in following chapter. In the process the questions raised in the previous chapter concerning the gains against poverty of women relative to the gains by men will again be encountered.

---

[2] _Ibid._, 29-30.

II: Previous Views on the Causes of the Feminization of
Poverty

Pearce explained the feminization of poverty largely
in terms of sex segregation in the labor market,
contending that "occupational ghettoization and
discrimination has prevented any improvement in women's
earnings relative to men."[3]   Similarly others who have
directly addressed the feminization of poverty imply that
it is the result of women's greater vulnerability to
poverty and that occupational segregation by sex
contributes to this enhanced vulnerability.[4]

Other researchers have arrived at the feminization
of poverty issue following discussions on divorce. These
studies tend to view the shift of poverty into FHHs as
the consequence of the increased incidence of divorce in
an economic and social environment that restrains the
economic viability of women. These restraints include
the laws concerning property settlements in divorce
cases, the responsibility of child care falling
disproportionately on mothers thereby yielding lower
labor force participation rates, and sex segregation in
the labor market. This view assumes that the changing

---

[3]Ibid., 45.

[4]This argument can be deduced from Smith (1986);
Stallard, Ehrenreich, and Sklar (1983); and Burnham
(1986).

demographics is the variable which has prompted the change in the degree of the feminization of poverty. That is, the economic and social restraints are described in relatively static terms as the setting in which the demographic consequences have been played out.

One little reported fact is the halt in the trend towards the feminization of poverty that occurred virtually at the moment that Pearce focused attention on the phenomenon. The data will be presented shortly which show that the share of total poverty suffered by individuals living in FHHs peaked in 1978. No one appears to have offered an explanation for this halt or the slight reversal in the trend that then followed. The previously posited "causes" of the phenomenon do not explain the reversal in the trend.

For example, if the feminization of poverty was caused by sex segregation in the labor market, did that segregation diminish, thereby reversing the trend towards the feminization of poverty? Sex segregation in the labor market will be addressed in detail in the following chapter. At this point let it suffice to note that studies on the phenomenon have concluded that sex segregation in the labor market has been largely maintained through the mid 1980s. Alternatively, if the feminization of poverty was caused by increased incidence of divorce in a relatively stable and hostile economic environment for women, did this demographic impetus stop, thereby causing the feminization trend to be altered? This seems implausible given the evidence in Chapter 2 that the incidence of divorce has remained at high levels. What then did cause the reversal in the feminization of poverty?

I develop an answer to this question beginning in the present chapter with a descriptive statistical analysis that separates the mathematical components of the measure of the feminization of poverty. In the following chapter an explanation of the feminization record is presented that links it to the other variable emphasized in this study: the composition of economic growth.

III: Mathematical Definition of the Feminization of Poverty

The feminization of poverty is the ratio of women's poverty to aggregate poverty. Hence, from the demographic perspective of sorting individuals by the sex of the households in which they live, the mathematical definition follows:

$$\frac{PFHH}{AP} = \tag{1}$$

$$\frac{PFHH}{PFHH + POHH} = \tag{2}$$

$$\frac{\left[\dfrac{FHHpop}{Apop} (Apop) \dfrac{PFHH}{FHHpop}\right]}{\left[\dfrac{FHHpop}{Apop} (Apop) \dfrac{PFHH}{FHHpop}\right] + \left[\dfrac{OHHpop}{Apop} (Apop) \dfrac{POHH}{OHHpop}\right]} \tag{3}$$

where PFHH = poor living in FHHs;
      AP = number of aggregate poor;
    POHH = poor living in OHHs;
  FHHpop = FHH population;
    Apop = aggregate population;
  OHHpop = OHH population.

In this way it is clear that the degree of the feminization of poverty depends upon the demographic composition of the population (i.e., [FHHpop/Apop] and [OHHpop/Apop]), the poverty rate among individuals living in female-headed households (PFHH/FHHpop), and the poverty rate among individuals in all other households (POHH/OHHpop). Ceteris paribus, a reduction (increase) in the poverty rate of FHHs will reduce (increase) the feminization of poverty. Other things equal, a reduction (increase) in the poverty rate of OHHs will increase (decrease) the feminization of poverty. Finally, other things equal, a shift of the population into (out of)

FHHs will increase (diminish) the feminization of poverty.

In the previous chapter poverty rates were viewed as independent of the demographic mix of the population. Here it will be further assumed that the poverty rates of the two demographic groups are independent of one another. Hence the close correlation between the poverty rates of these two demographic groups is assumed to reflect their common dependence on economic factors and not by causal links between the two.

Thus three factors emerge as independent determinants of the feminization of poverty. From this starting point I can statistically isolate the impact of the changing demographics and ascertain the extent to which the feminization of poverty is a consequence of the movement of the population into FHHs. Specifically I can address the questions: Has the feminization of poverty been primarily a consequence of a demographic phenomenon? To what extent have changing poverty rates reinforced or diminished the concentration of poverty among female-headed households?

IV: Relative Strength of the Determining Factors

The pattern of the feminization of poverty from 1959 through 1984 is given in Table 3.1, Column 1 and Figure 3.1.   The trend observed by Pearce continued only through 1979 and then was slightly reversed.

The   annual   changes   in   the   measure   of the feminization of poverty associated with each of its determining factors are provided in Columns 3, 4, and 5 of Table 3.1.   The net impacts over the entire period were also calculated and appear at the bottom of the Table.

The net impact associated with the change of the poverty rate of female-headed households was derived by first noting that in 1959, 11.7 percent of the population (Table 2.3, Column 3) and 26.3 percent of the poor lived in FHHs (Table 3.1, Column 1). The poverty rate for this group was   50.2   percent   (Table   2.3, Column 4). Hypothetically, had the demographic mix been unchanged and had the poverty rate of OHHs remained at its 1959 level, then in 1984, given the 1984 poverty rate for FHHs of 34 percent, 19.41 percent of the poor would have lived in households headed by women.   In fact, 49.06 percent of the poor lived in FHHs in 1984.   Consequently, the hypothetical decrease from 26.3 to 19.41 percent can be

Table 3.1: The feminization of poverty and its contributing factors

	(1)	(2)	(3)	(4)	(5)	(6)
	Percent of poor living in FHHs	Change in percent	Change due to change in FHH poverty rate	Change due to change in OHH poverty rate	Combined impact of change in FHH and OHH poverty rates	Change due to changed demographics
1959	26.31	–	–	–	–	–
1960	26.76	0.45	-0.27	0.21	-0.06	0.51
1961	27.25	0.49	0.00	0.43	0.43	0.06
1962	29.08	1.83	0.40	1.39	1.79	0.04
1963	30.46	1.38	-0.87	1.92	1.05	0.33
1964	30.43	-0.03	-1.11	0.41	-0.70	0.67
1965	33.32	2.89	0.05	2.92	2.97	-0.08
1966	35.95	2.63	-2.51	4.43	1.92	0.70
1967	38.14	2.19	-0.23	1.55	1.32	0.86
1968	40.82	2.68	-1.00	3.27	2.27	0.41
1969	43.12	2.30	-0.31	2.32	2.01	0.30
1970	43.88	0.76	-0.13	-0.60	-0.73	1.48
1971	44.64	0.76	-0.13	0.30	0.17	0.59
1972	47.37	2.73	-0.72	2.24	1.52	1.22
1973	49.44	2.07	-1.39	2.85	1.46	0.61
1974	47.88	-1.56	-0.95	-1.82	-2.77	1.21
1975	47.41	-0.47	0.73	-2.34	-1.61	1.14
1976	50.39	2.98	-0.14	2.35	2.21	0.78
1977	51.07	0.68	-1.19	0.71	-0.48	1.16
1978	52.58	1.51	-0.38	1.11	0.73	0.78
1979	51.79	-0.79	-0.23	-1.47	-1.70	0.91
1980	50.04	-1.75	1.36	-3.33	-1.97	0.22
1981	49.46	-0.58	1.01	-2.38	-1.37	0.79
1982	47.49	-1.97	0.70	-2.69	-1.99	0.01
1983	47.34	-0.15	-0.42	-0.75	-1.17	1.03
1984	49.06	1.72	-1.14	2.06	0.92	0.84
Net change from 1959-1984			-6.90	15.39	8.49	15.18

Source: Derived from Bureau of the Census P-60 Series, various years.

Figure 3.1: Percent of all poor living in female-headed households

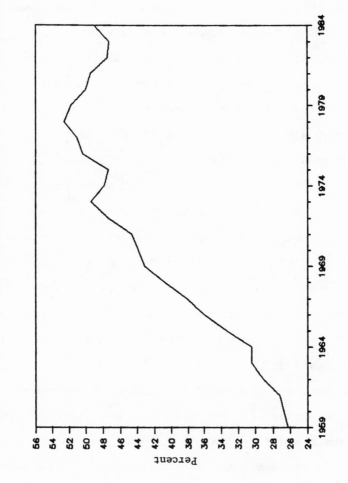

Source: Table 3.1, Column 1

attributed to the reduction in the poverty rates of female-headed households.

The effect of the changes in OHH poverty rate is calculated analogously by holding constant the FHH poverty rate and the demographic mix. Finally, the impact of the demographic shift is obtained by constraining both groups' poverty rates to the 1959 levels and observing the change in the feminization of poverty that would have occurred if only the demographic shift had taken place.

This procedure was repeated for each year over the time period and the results appear in Table 3.1. Positive numbers indicate an increase in the representation of individuals in FHHs among the poor, or the increased feminization of poverty. Negative signs indicate the opposite effect of the reduced feminization of poverty. The annual data are also presented in Figures 3.2 and 3.3.

In Figure 3.2 the separate impacts of the changes in the poverty rates of FHHs and OHHs are plotted. These are Columns 3 and 4 of Table 3.1. The two series worked as opposing forces generally throughout the 1960s when the declines in the poverty rates of FHHs worked to diminish the feminization of poverty and the declines in the poverty rates for OHHs operated to increase the

Figure 3.2: Impact of changing poverty rates on the ratio $\left[\dfrac{\text{Poor in female-headed households}}{\text{U.S. poor}}\right]$

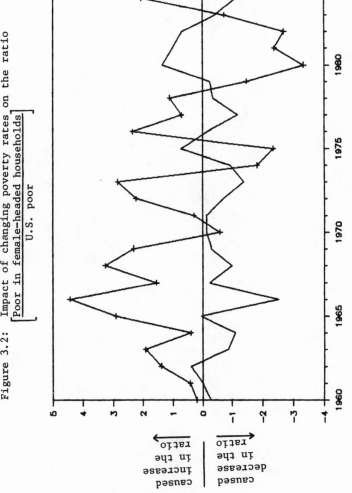

+ Impact of change in poverty rate of other headed households
− Impact of change in poverty rate of female-headed households

Source: Table 3.1, Columns 3 and 4

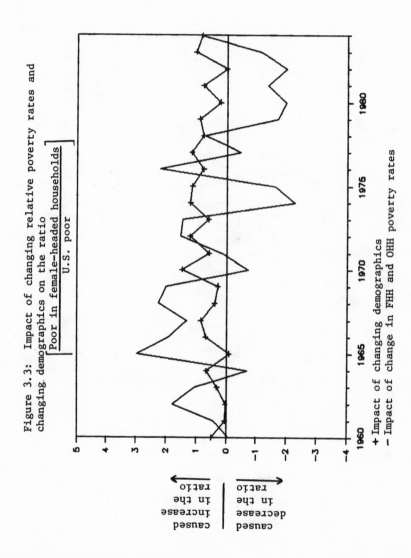

Figure 3.3: Impact of changing relative poverty rates and changing demographics on the ratio

Poor in female-headed households
—————————————————————————
U.S. poor

1960   1965   1970   1975   1980

+ Impact of changing demographics
− Impact of change in FHH and OHH poverty rates

Source: Table 3.1, Columns 5 and 6

feminization of poverty. The dominance of the OHH's impact yielded a net positive role of the combined effects of changes in the poverty rates. From 1980 through 1983 the two series again worked in clear opposition. However in those years the increases in the FHH poverty rate raised the feminization of poverty and the increases in the OHH poverty rate diminished the feminization of poverty. As in the 1960s the impact of the OHH poverty rates dominated.

This net or combined impact on the feminization of poverty of the changes in the poverty rates of the two groups appears in Table 3.1, Column 5, and is depicted as the solid line of Figure 3.3. As just described, in the 1960s the combined impact was generally positive and in the early 1980s it was negative, in both periods indicating that the effect of changes in poverty rates of OHHs was larger than the effect of changes in the FHH poverty rates. Although graphically the record of the 1970s is somewhat muddled, a glimpse along Columns 3 and 4 of Table 3.1 indicates that throughout the 1970s (except for 1977) the impact of the change in the OHH poverty rate was greater that the impact of the change in the FHH poverty rate.

This dominance of the impact of the OHH poverty rate reflects the fact previously noted: percentage changes in the poverty rates of OHHs exceeded the percentage changes in the poverty rates of FHHs. For example, the years in which the poverty rates worked together to reduce the feminization of poverty (1980 through 1983) were years in which the rates of both demographic groups were rising. However the poverty rate of the OHHs rose by greater percentages thereby contributing to a relative improvement for FHHs.

Figure 3.3 also presents the impact of the changed demographic mix. The demographic component generally operated throughout the period to increase the feminization of poverty. Finally the Figure allows a comparison of the relative strengths of the impact of the demographic factor and the combined impact of the changes in the poverty rates. That is, was the feminization of poverty primarily a demographic phenomenon?

It is apparent that the changing demographics worked relatively consistently throughout the period to increase the feminization of poverty. However the combined impact of the poverty rates was both comparatively strong and comparatively erratic. It worked in the earlier years to increase and later to decrease the feminization of poverty. Thus the feminization of poverty was not the simple consequence of the changing demographic mix but was also critically related to the relative changes in the poverty rates of female-headed households and all other households.

V: Women Bearing a Greater Portion of all Adult Poverty

The estimates of poverty among all adults provide a second indication of the recent pattern of the feminization of poverty. The degree of the concentration of women among the adult poor from 1959 through 1984 is indicated in Table 3.2 and Figure 3.4. Pearce's claim that as of her 1978 writing the group of adults living below the poverty line had been increasingly composed of women is generally substantiated by these findings. However it appears that the trend towards increased concentration of adult poverty among women occurred in the 1960s and early 1970s. In the mid 1970s the series shows little change.

Again due to limitations of the data, figures for the 1959 through 1973 period were estimated. Those estimates, the hatched line in Figure 3.4, suggest that in 1959 59.1 percent of the poor adult population was made up of females. Beginning in 1969 the Census estimates are available and are indicated by the solid line. According to this more dependable series, the feminization of poverty reached its highest level in 1973 and again in 1978. After 1978 there was a sharp reversal

Table 3.2:   Percent of adult poor that was female,
1959-1984

	Author's estimate	Census estimate
1959	59.1	na*
1960	59.5	na
1961	59.5	na
1962	59.9	na
1963	60.5	na
1964	61.1	na
1965	62.5	na
1966	62.8	na
1967	64.0	na
1968	64.4	na
1969	64.7	63.8
1970	65.0	64.4
1971	65.0	64.9
1972	66.2	65.5
1973	65.7	65.7
1974	na	64.7
1975	na	64.5
1976	na	65.3
1977	na	64.7
1978	na	65.7
1979	na	64.7
1980	na	64.5
1981	na	64.1
1982	na	62.2
1983	na	62.0
1984	na	62.1

* not available.

Source: See Appendix.

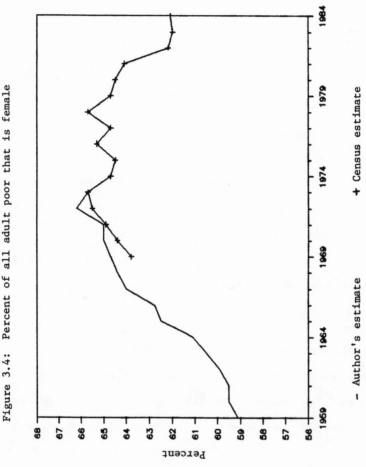

Figure 3.4: Percent of all adult poor that is female

– Author's estimate   + Census estimate

Source: Table 3.2

in the trend towards the feminization of poverty. Since throughout this period the demographic mix remained roughly constant with 52.5 percent of the adult population comprised of females, the explanation for this change in the trend must be attributed solely to differential changes in the poverty rates of women and men.

From Section VI of the previous chapter, which discussed the poverty rates of adult men and women, recall that the period of enhanced feminization of poverty (by this measure the 1960s and early 1970s) coincides with relatively greater progress against poverty by men than by women, and that the period of reduced feminization of poverty (the late 1970s and early 1980s) coincides with relatively smaller losses by women as compared to men.

VI: Specific Phenomenon to be Explained

No analysis will be aimed at explaining why the divorce rate increased and the population shifted into households headed by women. Rather efforts will be directed at explaining why women and FHHs enjoyed relatively smaller improvements against poverty in roughly the first two decades of the study period, but suffered smaller setbacks in the last years of the period.   These were the questions which emerged from the discussions in the previous   chapter (Sections   V and VI) concerning the   poverties of men and women, but also were the   key   to   an   understanding   of   the   pattern   of the feminization of poverty that arose from the discussion in Sections IV and V of the present chapter.

To   highlight   the   discrepancy   in   the   records of progress against poverty between female-headed households and all other households,   Table 3.3   is presented.   The trend towards   the increased   concentration of poverty in female-headed households peaked at 52.8 percent   in 1978. In the study period years prior to this peak, the poverty rate   of   female-headed   households   declined   from   50.2 percent to 32.3 percent, a 35.7 percent improvement.   The poverty rate of all other households over the   same years declined   from   18.7   to   6.6   percent,   a   64.7   percent improvement.   Over the remaining years of the period both groups   suffered   increases   in   their   poverty   rates. However, as   indicated in   Table 3.3,   OHHs experienced a larger percentage setback.

VII: Feminization   of   Poverty   as   a   Measure   of the Economic Status of Women

This chapter will conclude with an evaluation of the "feminization   of   poverty"   concept   as a measure of the

Table 3.3:   Percentage change in the poverty rate,
selected periods

	1959-1978	1979-1984
FHH	-35.7*	+6.3
OHH	-64.7	+32.9

* <u>(Poverty rate in 1959 - poverty rate in 1978)</u>
         Poverty rate in 1959

other statistics computed analogously.

Source: Derived from Table 2.3, and Bureau of the
Census, Current Population Reports, various years.

economic well-being of women.   Table 3.3 makes obvious
the problem with using the concept as a basis for judging
the economic status of women.   The feminization of
poverty increased from 1959 to 1978 at the same time that
the poverty rate of female-headed households diminished
by 35.7 percent.   The feminization of poverty declined
from 1979 to 1984 while the poverty rate of FHH
increased by 6.3 percent.   The difficulty, of course, is
that (demographics aside) the feminization of poverty
reflects the <u>relative</u> advances and setbacks of the two
groups against poverty.

        Once it is recognized in this light, the
appropriateness of the "feminization of poverty" as a

measure of the economic well-being of women is called into serious question. It is solely an indication of how women are doing relative to men and reflects not only changes in the relative poverty rates of the two demographic groups but also the demographic makeup of the economy.

However, the concept has prompted important questions into the discrepancy between women and men in the progress against poverty. It is to that issue that attention is now directed.

CHAPTER 4:

THE COMPOSITION OF ECONOMIC GROWTH

I: Introduction

Two broad sectors of the United States economy have received considerable recent attention from economists and policy makers.   These sectors are manufacturing and the services.   The services have been defined in a variety of ways to include some or all of the non-goods producing sectors of the economy. The present study will focus on the private service sectors[1] of transportation; communications; public utilities; wholesale trade; retail trade; finance, insurance and real estate; and "services[2]."

---

[1] I have elected to exclude the government services from our analysis.   This choice derived from the intent to evaluate the effectiveness of economic growth at reducing poverty, implicitly throughout the economic growth and poverty literature an evaluation of the "market" remedy for destitution.   By excluding the government sector the impact of the private sector is emphasized.

[2] Among the "services" are the industries of lodging places, personal services, business services, automotive repair, motion pictures, amusements, museums, and health, legal, educational, and private household services. "Services" along with retail trade emerge as dominant among all the private service industries. To distinguish the single sector of "services" from the umbrella designation of private services applied to all private non-goods producing industries, the former will be set off by quotation marks.

Consideration of manufacturing and/or the (variously defined) services has been included in discussions over a wide range of overlapping concerns including the incidence of plant closures and the problem of dislocated workers, the secular rise in the unemployment rate, the slowdown in the nation's productivity growth, the reduced ability of the United States to export, the role of women and minorities in the economy, the level of wages and the "disappearing" middle class, and the need for industrial policy. Here and in the following chapter the performance of the manufacturing and private service sectors will be linked to two additional phenomena: the feminization of poverty and the effectiveness of aggregate economic growth at alleviating poverty.

First it will be argued that growth in the private services renders aggregate economic growth a less potent anti-poverty weapon than does growth in the manufacturing sector. This leads to the hypothesis that the relative output levels of manufacturing and the private services influence the anti-poverty effectiveness of economic growth.

Then the focus will shift to the role that women play in the U.S. market economy. It will be demonstrated that this pattern of women's employment combined with the recent pattern of economic growth helps answer the

questions which emerged in the two previous chapters:
Why are women's poverty rates higher than men's poverty
rates? Why did women and men experience different
patterns of progress against poverty in the 1960s through
the early 1980s? Hence insights will be gained into the
causes of the feminization of poverty in the 1960s and
1970s and the reduced feminization of poverty of the
early 1980s.

II: Why the Composition of Growth Matters

Growth in the private service industries is held to
be less effective at reducing poverty than is growth in
manufacturing because employment in the two sectors is
typically very different. When compared to employment in
manufacturing, employment in the private services
generally pays less per hour, is more likely to be part-
time, and is more likely to be intermittent. Furthermore
since 1965 the discrepancy in the hourly wages of workers
in the two sectors has increased and the discrepancy in
the average number of hours worked per week has
broadened. These observations have important
implications for the anti-poverty effectiveness of
aggregate economic growth. The evidence in support of
these distinctions in employment between the sectors will
be reviewed.

It is first important to recognize that employment within the private service industries is dominated by employment in retail trade and in the "services." Also due to disproportionate growth in "services" employment, the dominance of retail trade and "services" has increased since 1965. See Table 4.1. In 1985 approximately 70 percent of all private service jobs were in one of these industries. The significance of this distribution of private service jobs is that among all private service industries, retail trade and "services" consistently pay the lowest average hourly wages and have the shortest average work weeks.

Table 4.2 presents for 1965, 1975, and 1985 the average hourly earnings among employees in all private service industries, and separately for workers in the retail, "service," and manufacturing industries. The Table also indicates the sectors' earnings as a percentage of earnings in manufacturing. Private service hourly earnings as a percentage of manufacturing earnings declined over each decade. This reflects both the decline in the relative wage of retail workers and (as shown in Table 4.1) the relative increase in the percentage of all workers who work in the "services," consistently second only to retail in lowest average hourly earnings.

Table 4.1:   Retail and "service" jobs as a percentage of
total private service employment

	1965	1975	1985
Retail	32.2	31.9	30.9
"Services"	31.4	35.0	39.1
Retail plus "services"	63.6	66.9	69.9

Source: U.S. Department of Labor,   _Employment and Earnings_, vol. 34, no. 7 (July 1987), Table B-1.   In

addition to typically earning less per hour than manufacturing workers, private service workers on average work fewer hours per week. This discrepancy too has increased over time. Table 4.3 indicates that in 1975 the average work week of all private service workers had dropped below 35 hours, a common definition for "part-time" employment.[3] In 1985 the typical work week for the private service sector had declined to 33.2 hours. As indicated, workers in retail sales and the "services" typically worked even less while the average manufacturing work week remained consistently close to 40 hours per week.

_____

[3]For example, this definition of "part-time" employment is used by Shirley J. Smith, "Work Experience of the Labor Force During 1985," _Monthly Labor Review_, 110, no. 4 (April, 1987), 41.

Table 4.2: Average hourly earnings of selected non-supervisory workers

	Average hourly earnings		
	1965	1975	1985
All private service employees	$2.22	4.11	7.75
Retail	1.82	3.36	5.94
"Services"	2.05	4.02	7.89
Manufacturing	2.50	4.83	9.53

	Percentage of manufacturing hourly earnings		
	1965	1975	1985
All private service employees	88.8	85.1	81.3
Retail	72.8	70.0	62.3
"Services"	82.0	83.2	82.8

Source: U.S. Department of Labor, _Employment and Earnings_, vol. 28, no. 3 (March 1981), Table C-1; vol.34, no. 3 (March 1987), Table C-1.

Table 4.3:   Average work week in hours

	Average work week		
	1965	1975	1985
All private service employees	37.6	34.8	33.2
Retail	36.6	32.4	29.4
"Services"	35.9	33.5	32.5
Manufacturing	41.2	39.5	40.5

	Percentage of manufacturing work week		
	1965	1975	1985
All private service employees	91.3	88.1	82.0
Retail	88.8	82.0	72.6
"Services"	87.1	84.8	80.2

Source: U.S. Department of Labor, _Employment and Earnings_, vol. 28, no. 3 (March 1981), Table C-1; vol.34, no. 3 (March 1987), Table C-1.

Other researchers have concluded that the intermittency of employment is higher in the service industries. Based on 1978 Current Population Survey data, Sekscenski observed that the average length of job tenure for men in trade, "services," and manufacturing was 2.5, 3.5, and 5.0 years respectively while for women the job tenures were 1.5, 2.6, and 3.5 years respectively. Hence there was a gap between job tenure in manufacturing and the sectors dominant among the private services.[4] Miller and Tomaskovic-Dewey attributed the relative instability of employment in the services to the instability of the typical service firm. They maintained that the "service industries are populated by small firms that tend to be unstable. Competition is fierce and employment is unstable."[5] Smith also posited that the high degree of competitiveness in the services industries renders the service sector employment irregular.[6]

---

[4]Edward Sekscenski, "Job Tenure Declines as Work Force Changes," Monthly Labor Review, 102 no. 12 (December 1979), 48-50.

[5]S.M. Miller and Donald Tomaskovic-Dewey, Recapitalizing America (Boston: Routledge and Kegan Paul, 1986) 30.

[6]Joan Smith, "The Paradox of Women's Poverty: Wage-earning Women and Economic Transformation," in Women and Poverty, ed. by Clare C. Novak and Myra H. Strober, (Chicago: The University of Chicago Press, 1986), 121-

In sum, growth in the private service sector, when compared to growth in manufacturing, yields lower paying, more part-time, and more intermittent employment. Consequently aggregate economic growth is expected to be more or less effective at reducing poverty depending upon the sectoral composition of growth. When manufacturing growth contributes relatively heavily to aggregate growth, aggregate growth is expected to be a more potent anti-poverty force than when the contribution of private services is more dominant.

III: Sex Segregation by Occupation

Two different perspectives on sex segregation in the labor market will be presented in this and the following section. They are occupational segregation by sex and segregation by major industrial category. Together they explain very much about why women are more impoverished than men and why the two sexes have experienced different patterns of change in their poverty rates.

Sex segregation in the labor market, or occupational segregation by sex, is the "concentration of men and women in different jobs that are predominantly of a

---

140.

single sex."[7] The conclusion widely drawn by scholars of
this phenomenon is that relative to men, women are more
concentrated in lower paying jobs.   Those who have
extended the analysis to the consideration of poverty
have commonly held that sex segregation in the labor
market has contributed to the greater impoverishment of
women.[8]

Evidence to support the existence of sex segregation
in the labor market and to demonstrate that the
segregation operates to the relative detriment of women
workers, has been presented in myriad forms. A small
portion of that evidence will be reproduced here.

One clear indication was provided by Mellor and
Stamas who selected from the 46 industrial groups in the
private sector the six highest paying and the six lowest
paying industries. For each of these twelve industries
they reported the median weekly earnings and the percent
of the workers that was female. Their results, presented
in Table 4.4, indicate that each of the six highest paid
industries have below-average proportions of women

---

[7]Barbara F. Reskin and Heidi I. Hartmann, Women's
Work, Men's Work: Sex Segregation on the Job,
(Washington D.C.: National Academy Press, 1986).

[8]This has been the conclusion drawn by the U.S.
Department of Labor, Women's Bureau (1983); Pearce
(1978); Smith (1986); Stallard, Ehrenreich, and Sklar
(1983); and others.

Table 4.4: Highest and lowest paying industries, median weekly earnings, and percent of workers who are women, 1980

	Median weekly earnings	Percent who are women
All full-time workers	$289	39
Highest-paying industries:		
Petroleum and coal products	433	20
Mining	423	15
Railroad transportation	422	7
Aircraft and parts manufacture	414	23
Ordinance	410	22
Motor vehicle and equipment manufacture	407	15
Lowest-paying industries:		
Agriculture	189	16
Personal services	188	59
Leather and leather products	185	61
Eating and drinking places	174	55
Apparel manufacture	170	79
Private households	114	90

Source: Mellor and Stamas (1982), 19.

employees, while the lowest paid industries, with only one exception, have above-average proportions of women workers.

A more comprehensive perspective on the differences in the occupations and earnings of women and men is the distribution of each gender across the major occupational groups. As evidenced in Table 4.5, over half of all women employees held jobs either in clerical or service positions, while the majority of men were employed in the higher paying occupations as craft workers, professional and technical workers, and managers.

It is also clear that within each occupation men were better paid than women. To an extent this earnings discrepancy reflected further sex segregation within the occupations. For example, within the category of professional and technical jobs, 52 percent of the women were employed either as teachers (except college) or as nurses, dieticians, and therapists. The median weekly earnings of all teachers was $333 and for the group of health care workers it was $327. Professional men were much more likely than professional women to work in the higher paying occupations (earnings in parentheses) of engineer ($540), computer specialist ($454), lawyer and judge ($550), and physician, dentist, and related practitioner ($468). Similarly among salesworkers, over

Table 4.5: Major occupation groups of employed persons and associated median weekly earnings of full-time wage and salary workers, by sex, 1981

	Occupational distribution		Median weekly earnings	
	Women	Men	Women	Men
White collar workers	65.9	42.9	$316	$439
Professional and technical	17.0	15.9		
Managers and administrators (except farm)	7.4	14.6	283	466
Sales	6.8	6.1	190	366
Clerical	34.7	6.3	220	328
Blue collar workers	13.6	20.7		
Craft and kindred	1.9	20.7	239	360
Operatives (except transport)	9.7	11.1	187	298
Transport equipment operatives	0.7	5.5	237	244
Nonfarm laborers	1.2	7.1	165	238
Service workers	19.4	8.9	165	238
Farm workers	1.1	3.9	148	183
Total	100.0	100.0	224	347

Source: Employment data from U.S. Department of Labor (1983), Table II-1; earnings data from Rytina (1982), Table 1.

half the women worked in the lowest paid group of retail salesclerk where median earnings were $178, while the largest single group among male salesworkers comprising 28 percent of this male group, was that of wholesale trade representative, with median weekly earnings of $396.[9]

The summary statistic widely employed to represent the earnings discrepancy between male and female full-time year-round workers is that on average, women earn 60 cents for every $1.00 earned by men. This ratio has held almost constant for at least the last 25 years.[10]

Not only were women's median earnings lower than men's, but as would be expected, their entire earnings distribution was lower than that of men. This served to swell the female representation among low paid workers

---

[9]Nancy F. Rytina, "Earnings of Men and Women: A Look at Specific Occupations," Monthly Labor Review, (April, 1982), 25-31.

[10]Among those who have made this observation are The Department of Labor (1983), Reskin and Hartmann (p. 10), Blau and Ferber (pp. 170-171), and Corcoran, Duncan, and Hill (pp. 8-9). The latter note that the modern persistence of valuing women's work at about three-fifths of that of men has biblical backing: "The Lord spoke to Moses and said, 'When a man makes a special vow to the Lord which required your valuation of living persons, a male between twenty and sixty years old shall be values at fifty shekels. If it is a female, she shall be valued at thirty shekels.'" -Lev. 27:1-4.

and left women under represented among higher paid
workers. This is depicted in Table 4.6. While we do not
know how many of the men and women in the lower end of
the cumulative distributions depended on their
individual earnings as the sole source of market income,
it is both reasonable and common to attribute the greater
incidence of poverty among women to the greater
concentration of women workers at the lower end of the
earnings scale.[11] To support this presumption it can be
noted that in 1981 the poverty rate among people living
in FHHs with a full-time year-round employed head was
6.9 percent. The rate for the comparable group living
in all other households was 3.1 percent.[12]

Two recent studies surveyed the literature on the
historic patterns of sex segregation in the labor market.
Reskin and Hartmann observed that "[t]he overall degree
of sex segregation has been a remarkably stable
phenomenon; it has not changed much since at least
1900."[13] Blau and Ferber drew the same conclusion:
"There is no reason to question the unanimous findings of
the studies on this subject, all of which point to little

[11]See footnote 7.

[12]Bureau of the Census, Current Population Reports
P-60 Series, No. 138.

[13]Reskin and Hartmann (1986), 1.

Table 4.6: Earnings distribution of year-round full-time workers, by sex, 1981, persons 15 years of age and over

Earnings group	Distribution		Cumulative Distribution	
	Women	Men	Women	Men
Less than $3,000	2.3	2.5	2.3	2.5
$3,000 to $4,999	2.5	1.1	4.8	3.6
$5,000 to $6,999	6.9	2.7	11.7	6.3
$7,000 to $9,999	20.3	6.5	32.0	12.8
$10,000 to $14,999	35.1	17.8	67.1	30.6
$15,000 to $24,999	27.7	35.9	94.8	66.5
$25,000 to $49,999	5.0	28.7	99.8	95.2
$50,000 to $74,999	0.1	3.2	99.9	98.4
$75,000 and over	0.1	1.5	100.0	100.0
Total	100.0	100.0		

Source: U.S. Department of Labor (1983), Table III-3.

change over a number of decades."[14] The consequences of sex segregation have likewise been dependable. The steady earnings differential between full-time year-round male and female workers has previously been cited. Not as well recognized is the rough consistency of the ratio of poverty rate of individuals living in female-headed families with a full-time year-round working head to the poverty rate for those living in all other families with a full-time year-round working head. In the 1960s, these female-headed families were 2.44 times as likely to be poor, and in the 1970s, 2.54 times as likely to live below the poverty line. From 1980 through 1985, the ratio has averaged 2.08.[15]

In sum, the existing occupational segregation by sex is held to contribute to the higher rates of impoverishment of women. Hence we begin to answer the questions raised in the previous two chapters on the poverty of women and the poverty of women relative to the poverty of men.

---

[14]Francine D. Blau and Marianne A. Ferber, The Economics of Women, Men, and Work (Englewood Cliffs, New Jersey: Prentice-Hall, 1986), 166. Blau actually contributed to this literature and found a slight reduction in the degree of sex segregation in the 1970s. See Blau and Hendricks, (1979).

[15]Bureau of the Census, Current Population Reports P-60 Series, various years.

IV: Sex Segregation by Major Industrial Category

Section II referred to the current wide attention being given to the shift in the sectoral composition of the U.S. economic activity. The two sectors which have been scrutinized are the services and manufacturing. This dichotomy will again be used as the broad framework for analysis.

In order to relate the poverties of women and men to the composition of economic growth, it is important to recognize the sex distribution of workers over the major (nonagricultural) industrial categories. This perspective on labor market segregation is provided in Table 4.7. In general women are more highly concentrated in the lower paid private service industries especially in the lowest paid industries of retail trade; finance, insurance, and real estate; and "services." Alternatively, men are less concentrated in the private service industries and are more likely than women to be in the goods producing sector, especially the relatively high paying manufacturing industry. Given this division of the labor force by sex into different industries, the importance of the composition of economic growth becomes apparent.

Table 4.7: Sex distribution over major industrial categories for nonagricultural industries, October 1984, and associated average weekly earnings of production for nonsupervisory workers for 1984

Industry division	Percent of all women in this industry	Percent of all employees female	Percent of all men in this industry	Actual earnings
Mining	0.3	12.2	1.7	$503.58
Construction	1.0	9.5	7.9	456.92
Manufacturing	15.1	32.4	25.2	376.63
Transportation and public utilities	3.4	27.2	7.2	437.73
Wholesale trade	3.8	28.5	7.6	345.86
Retail trade	20.1	51.9	15.0	176.40
Fire, insurance, and real estate	8.1	60.7	4.2	278.13
Services	29.4	59.9	15.9	250.59

Source: Employment data is presented by Reskin and Hartmann (1986), Table 2-3; the earnings data is from Monthly Labor Review (March 1986), Table 16.

As previously noted, recent discussions of the
structure of economic growth have centered on the
relative decline of manufacturing output and the relative
increase in the production of private services. Table
4.8 indicates the manufacturing output per capita and the
private services output per capita over the 1959 to 1984
period. Further, the Table and Figure 4.1 present the
ratio of manufacturing output to private service output.
This ratio reached its peak in 1966 and then generally
declined through the end of the period.

Table 4.9 provides an alternative perspective on the
relative decline in manufacturing output. It indicates
substantial per capita growth in both the private
services industries and in manufacturing in the 1960s.
These per capita growth figures represented large
percentage improvements over the record of the 1950s.
The per capita growth in private services increased by
even more in the 1970s and though it declined from that
high level over the 1980-1984 period, it did then
maintain the growth level of the 1960s. Per capita
output in manufacturing also continued to increase, but
the amount of the increase dwindled over each time
period. The much reduced average per capita increase in
the 1980s reflects in part the deep recession of the

Table 4.8:   Manufacturing and private services output per
capita (1972 doaalars)

Year	Manufacturing output per capita	Private services output per capita	Ratio of manufacturing output to private services output
1959	$963	$1969	0.49
1960	951	1999	0.48
1961	936	2021	0.46
1962	1001	2098	0.48
1963	1068	2150	0.50
1964	1129	2231	0.51
1965	1218	2332	0.52
1966	1297	2435	0.53
1967	1280	2497	0.51
1968	1336	2604	0.51
1969	1368	2679	0.51
1970	1274	2701	0.47
1971	1285	2766	0.46
1972	1394	2906	0.48
1973	1535	3038	0.51
1974	1458	3046	0.48
1975	1341	3054	0.44
1976	1456	3157	0.46
1977	1540	3304	0.47
1978	1605	3463	0.46
1979	1631	3568	0.46
1980	1541	3558	0.43
1981	1564	3637	0.43
1982	1449	3603	0.40
1983	1510	3707	0.41
1984	1653	3925	0.42

Source: CITIBASE: Citibank economic   database [machine-
readable   magnetic   data   file].   1946-1984.   New York,
Citibank, N.A. 1978.

Figure 4.1:   Manufacturing output/Private services output

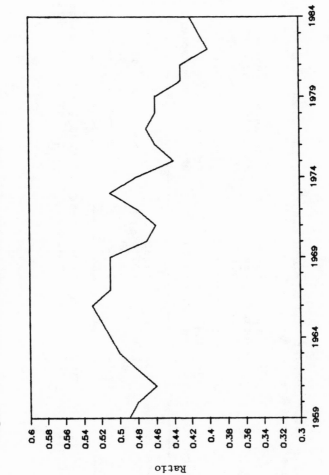

Source: Table 4.8

Table 4.9: Private service and manufacturing output per capita, levels and trends

Years	Average per capita growth in output		Percentage change from previous time period	
	Private services	Manufacturing	Private services	Manufacturing
1948-1958	$38.42	19.12	-	-
1959-1969	71.04	40.50	85	118
1970-1979	88.89	26.30	25	-35
1980-1984	71.33	4.43	-20	-83

Source: CITIBASE: Citibank economic database [machine-readable magnetic data file]. 1946-1984. New York, Citibank, N.A. 1978.

early 1980s.   (In   1982 manufacturing   output per capita
dropped over \$114.[16].)

V: Women and the Growth of Services

Michael Urquhart[17]   recently   argued   that   the most
dominant feature   of the   relative shift of employment to
the service sector is that the new service jobs are to a
great   extent   being   filled   by women entering the labor
force.   His   analysis   was   based   on   an   examination of
employment   status   in   1977   and   1978   of   the   60,000
households   in   the   Current   Population   Survey   sample.
Among   his   observations   were   that   14.5 percent of the
service workers in 1978 did not   work in   that sector the
previous year   and of those who joined the service sector
over 60 percent entered from outside of the   labor force.
He next   examined all those who were employed in 1978 and
not employed in 1977 and   found   that   nearly   78 percent
worked   in   services.   Among the new women workers 83.2
percent worked in the services, while   among the   new men
workers,   64.9   percent   worked   in   the   services.

---

[16]CITIBASE: Citibank   economic   database [machine-
readable magnetic data file].   1946-1984.   New York, N.A.
1978.

[17]Michael   Urquhart,   "The   Employment   Shift   to
Services: Where Did It Come From?"   Monthly Labor Review
(April, 1984), 15-22.

Furthermore, three-quarters of all entrants were women. These facts contributed to Urquhart's conclusion that "the primary source of new employees in the service sector was the employment of women who had previously not held jobs."[18]

Joan Smith presented an analysis on the same theme.[19] Considering the 1970s, Smith argued that "most available new jobs offer workers little chance to climb out of poverty. The vast majority of these positions are in the rapidly expanding service sector of the economy and are occupied predominantly by women."[20] Smith specifically examined the relationship between the growth of the service sector and the increased labor force participation of women. She posited that these developments, though independently caused, "have combined to create a paradoxical situation for U.S. women today." She maintained that the private services were able to "expand as rapidly as they have almost exclusively because women have been willing to take work that is less than desirable." Thus the paradox that despite their central role in the economic expansion, women "still

---

[18]Ibid., 21.

[19]See footnote 6.

[20]Ibid., 121.

receive the lowest pay and are subject to the least desirable employment practices."[21]

The central point is that the concurrent increased labor force participation of women and the growth in the types of jobs that women have traditionally held, combined to contribute to the preservation of the status quo for women in the labor market. Sex segregation and its consequent lower earnings and higher poverty rates for women were largely maintained throughout the period.

VI: Extent of Labor Force Participation

Another critical factor contributing to the higher absolute poverty levels of women is the lower propensity of these heads to be in the labor market, and among those in the market, a lower propensity to work either full-time or year-round. This characteristic of women's employment is complimentary to our propensity to work in the more typically part-time and intermittent positions in the "services."

Table 4.10 contrasts the labor force participation of male and female heads of households. In 1979 63.3 percent of the female heads of households worked in the

---

[21] Ibid., 121-122.

Table 4.10:   Labor force participation and poverty rates for
female-headed and other-headed households, 1969 and 1979

| | 1969 | | 1979 | |
	FHHs	OHHs	FHHs	OHHs
Total (in thousands)	5,581	45,656	8,540	49,886
Labor force participation (percentages)				
Head worked during the year	59.4	87.2	63.3	82.0
Of those who worked:				
full-time workers	79.1	94.8	80.3	93.8
of the full-time workers:				
worked 50-52 weeks	66.2	84.1	70.5	83.3
worked 1-49 weeks	33.8	15.9	29.5	16.7
part-time workers	20.9	5.2	19.7	6.2
Of the part-time workers:				
worked 50-52 weeks	38.2	42.3	39.5	42.0
worked 1-49 weeks	61.8	57.7	60.5	58.0
Poverty rates of families				
All families	32.3	6.9	30.2	5.5
Head worked during the year	23.3	4.9	18.9	3.8
Of those who worked:				
full-time workers	18.1	4.0	14.0	3.5
Of the full-time workers:				
worked 50-52 weeks	8.3	2.9	5.4	2.2
worked 1-49 weeks	37.4	9.9	34.7	9.8
part-time workers	42.7	19.9	39.1	9.2
Of the part-time workers:				
worked 50-52 weeks	32.1	15.8	25.5	6.5
worked 1-49 weeks	49.2	22.9	47.9	11.2

Source: Current Population Reports, P-60 Series, Nos. 76 and
130.

market place. Of that group roughly four-fifths (80.3 percent) worked full-time and of the full-time working female heads, 70.5 percent worked year-round. Thus approximately 36 percent (63.3 percent times 80.3 percent times 70.5 percent) of all female heads of households worked full-time and year-round. In all other households 82 percent of the heads participated in the labor force. Of that group almost 94 percent worked full-time and of the full-time workers 83.3 percent worked year-round. Hence 64 percent (0.82 times 0.938 times 0.833) of the heads of all other households worked full-time and year-round.

Table 4.10 also supports the perception that sex segregation in the labor market works to the economic disadvantage of women. As illustrated, for each category of time devoted to work in the marketplace by the heads of households, households with female heads suffered higher poverty rates than did all other households. For example, among the FHHs whose head worked full-time and year-round in 1979 the poverty rate was 5.4 percent while for OHH it was 2.2 percent.

Finally Table 4.10 indicates that the labor force participation of women heads of households increased from 1969 to 1979. Table 4.11 is provided to expand this point. It reports the labor force participation rates of

Table 4.11:   Labor   force participation   rates of women,
1950-1984

	Percent of women in the labor force	Increase over previous decade
1950	33.9	—
1960	37.8	3.9
1970	43.4	5.5
1980	51.6	8.3
1984	53.6	2.0*

* Increase since 1980.

Source: Blau and Ferber (1986), Table 4.1.

all women for selected years 1950 through 1984 and
clearly demonstrates the well recognized significant
increase in these rates.   Thus women have become
increasingly involved in the labor force, the trend that
was pointed out by the studies of Urquhart and Smith.

VII: The Composition of Economic Growth and the Poverty
Rates of Women and Men

One can now fit together a framework which describes
how the composition of economic growth has contributed to
the discrepancy in the progress against poverty made by
women and men. Fundamentally, men and women are viewed
as typically having different market experiences. Women
have been relatively isolated in the private services, a

sector which over the study period has experienced steady performance in comparison to manufacturing.[22]

Growth in the private services has been accompanied by increases in the labor force participation of women. However, wages have remained low and the increased employment has yielded (relative to men) only moderate reductions in the poverty of women and FHHs. Thus, women workers have been concentrated in low paying, but less volatile industries in the private services and their gains against poverty in the early part of the study period were not proportionately as great as those of men and OHHs. This perspective also offers an insight to the relatively smaller setbacks of FHHs in the latter part of the period: women's labor market seclusion in the relatively stable industries left them less vulnerable to fluctuations in the aggregate economy in the late 1970s and early 1980s.

As has been described, men more typically work in the higher paying but more volatile manufacturing sector.

---

[22]This "steady performance in comparison to manufacturing" (and later "less volatile") characterization of the private services refers to the output levels of the sectors as a whole. See again Table 4.9. While individual establishments within the private services have been characterized as unstable when compared to establishments in the manufacturing sector, the total output level of the private services has been less volatile than the total output level of manufacturing.

Thus in the years of high growth in manufacturing, men and OHHs enjoyed greater progress against poverty. However in the late 1970s and early 1980s when the economy experienced recession, the male-concentrated manufacturing sector was hit harder causing men and OHHs to suffer relatively greater setbacks against poverty.

In this framework women are viewed as operating in a more stable but more impoverished economic environment. They are seen to work in the less volatile private services but earning wages insufficient to march them by large strides out of poverty.

Alternatively, the economic well-being of men and OHHs is relatively more volatile because these workers are more closely linked to the less stable but higher paying manufacturing sector. When manufacturing thrives, as in the 1960s, the high wages are very effective at reducing poverty. However when manufacturing output lapses, as in the recession of the early 1980s, OHH poverty rates are again very responsive.

In sum, given the pattern of sex segregation in the labor market, the composition of economic growth emerges as a factor explaining the discrepancy in the progress against poverty of FHHs and OHHs. Consequently, it is also a factor contributing to the level of the feminization of poverty. That is, the potency of economic growth at reducing the poverty rates of OHHs and FHHs depends upon the sectors in which the growth occurs. Finally, the relative change in the poverty rates of the two demographic groups impacts the degree of the feminization of poverty.

VIII: Qualified Econometric Support

The difficulties of modeling econometrically the causes of poverty are vast. The list of causes is long, the "explanatory" variables are often highly correlated, and the possibility exists that poverty breeds the conditions that lead to more poverty (i.e., yielding the problem of assigning causation). Hence, in the study of the causes of poverty, precise empirical support is usually unavailable.

Accordingly no model will be posited as the "true" model explaining the change in the poverty rates of FHHs and OHHs. However, econometric methods may be used to support the thesis of this chapter that the composition of economic growth is a concern relevant to the discussion of the separate poverty of men and women.

Qualified econometric evidence is available to support the theory that the growth in manufacturing and the growth in private services differentially impact the poverty of FHHs and OHHs. The evidence will support the posited explanation of the increase and later decrease in the feminization of poverty. The following equation was estimated for FHHs and OHHs:

$$\% \triangle P = a + b \ (MANpcg) + c \ (PSpcg) \tag{1}$$

where P = poverty rate;
MANpcg = manufacturing per capita growth;
and PSpcg = private services per capita growth.

The percentage change in the poverty rate was employed as the dependent variable because, demographics aside, differences in the percentage improvement in the poverty rate for each sex change the degree of the feminization of poverty. For example, when men enjoy larger percentage improvements in their poverty rate relative to women, the feminization of poverty increases. Alternatively, when women suffer a smaller increase in their poverty rates relative to the increase realized by men, the feminization of poverty diminishes.

The results for the 1960 to 1984 time period appear in Table 4.12. These results generally support the posited theory. The results for OHHs indicate that only growth in the manufacturing sector significantly impacted the poverty rate for this group. Given the linear specification of the equation, the expected negative sign

Table 4.12:   Regression results for Equation 1

	Parameter estimate (t-statistic)			
Type of household	MANpcg	PSpcg	R-squared	DW
FHH	−0.002 (−1.26)	−0.0000 (−0.27)	0.32	2.06
OHH	−0.0009* (−3.92)	0.0002 (0.69)	0.79	2.27^

* Statistically significant at 95% level of confidence
^ Corrected for autocorrelation using Cochrane-Orcutt

procedure relates changes in manufacturing output
indirectly to changes in the poverty rate.

The results for FHHs actually are even more dismal
than the theory previously presented.   The economic
activity of neither sector was significantly related to
changes in the poverty rate.   In part this reflects the
relatively smaller dependent variable values.   Since the
observed percentage changes in the poverty rate for FHHs
were smaller,   it   was   more   difficult   to obtain
statistical significance from the same set of explanatory
variables.   Interesting, too, is the low R-squared.

The lack of significant coefficient estimates and
the low R-squared for FHHs can be interpreted to indicate
that the percentage changes in the poverty rates of FHHs

are not tightly linked to economic growth, regardless of the sector in which the growth occurs. That is, since women are more likely found in low paying, part-time and intermittent jobs and as a group have lower labor force participation rates, their poverty rates are not expected to be responsive even to a thriving economy. Non-market factors are likely critical determinants of the poverty rates of FHHs. A list of such factors would include the level of government transfers, the amount and reliability of child support payments, and the availability of child care.

IX: Summary

The second factor held to reduce the anti-poverty impact of economic growth is the shift of output out of manufacturing into the private service industries. Relative to manufacturing employment, the jobs in the private services typically pay less per hour and are more likely part-time and intermittent positions.

Answers were then developed to the questions raised in Chapters 2 and 3. Those questions were: Why are women's poverty rates higher than men's poverty rates? Compared to men why did women experience smaller percentage improvements in their poverty rates in the

1960s and early 1970s, but smaller percentage increases in their poverty rates in the early 1980s?

Two widely recognized factors which contribute to women's higher poverty rates are occupational segregation by sex and women's lower labor force participation rates. Female family heads typically work less than male family heads and women's market efforts are concentrated in typically lower paying jobs. There is also an evident pattern of industrial segregation by sex with women concentrated in the lower paying private service industries and men more likely to work in higher paying manufacturing jobs. Two studies were noted which observed that the growth in the production of the services has been accompanied by (and perhaps even allowed by) the increased labor force participation of women.

The pattern of sex segregation in the labor market combined with the patterns of output in the private services and manufacturing to yield an explanation for the varied records of progress against poverty for men and women. In the 1960s and early 1970s growth in the private services helped women emerge from poverty. However, growth in the higher paying manufacturing sector helped reduce the poverty rate of men by even larger percentages. These were years in which the feminization of poverty increased reflecting that the percentage improvement in women's poverty rates were smaller than those of men. In the early 1980s growth in the manufacturing sector slowed dramatically and in some years this output actually declined. This caused increases in the poverty of men. During these years the private service output was less volatile and the poverty rates of women rose less dramatically. Hence women gained relative to men and the feminization of poverty was reversed.

CHAPTER 5:

THE DIMINISHED ANTI-POVERTY EFFECT OF ECONOMIC GROWTH

I: Introduction

The literature review of Chapter 1 concluded that in evaluating the effect of economic growth as a remedy for poverty, it is important to recognize factors which impact the relationship between growth and poverty reduction.   If those factors change over time, then the reliability of growth as an anti-poverty weapon also will vary.   Two factors which do impact the anti-poverty effect of economic growth are the rate of divorce and the sectoral composition of growth.

As discussed in Chapter 2, divorce increases the population which has historically benefitted less from economic growth. This is the group of households that is headed by women. These people are more likely to be poor for reasons including sex segregation in the labor market, insufficient and unreliable child support payments, and shortages of affordable day care for children. Consequently, as the divorce rate increases economic growth becomes a less viable instrument against poverty.

Chapter 4 of this dissertation offered that the shift of the economy toward private service output has also reduced the anti-poverty impact of aggregate economic growth. Compared to employment in manufacturing, jobs in the private service sectors typically pay less per hour and are more likely to be part-time and intermittent positions. Hence these jobs are less effective at pulling workers over the official poverty line.

In this final chapter a model is developed to test these hypotheses. The model will also be employed to project the future impact of growth on poverty.

II: The Data on Divorce

Estimates of the number of divorces were presented in Chapter 2, Table 2.2. Two additional perspectives on the divorce trend are provided in Table 5.1. These are the rate of divorce per 1,000 total population and the rate of divorce per 1,000 married women over the age of 15. These two rates of divorce are also depicted in Figure 5.1.

The growth in the magnitude of divorce is indicated best by the growth in the rate of divorce per 1,000 total population. Each of the other indices could fail to accurately reflect the increased prevalence of divorce in the population at large. That is, the growth in the number of divorces provided in Table 2.2 may simply

Table 5.1: Estimated rates of divorce

Year	(1) Rate of divorce per 1,000 total population	(2) Rate of divorce per 1,000 married women 15 years of age and older
1959	2.2	9.3
1960	2.2	9.2
1961	2.3	9.6
1962	2.2	9.4
1963	2.3	9.6
1964	2.4	10.0
1965	2.5	10.6
1966	2.5	10.9
1967	2.6	11.2
1968	2.9	12.5
1969	3.2	13.4
1970	3.5	14.9
1971	3.7	15.8
1972	4.0	17.0
1973	4.3	18.2
1974	4.6	19.3
1975	4.8	20.3
1976	5.0	21.1
1977	5.0	21.1
1978	5.1	21.9
1979	5.3	22.8
1980	5.2	22.6
1981	5.3	22.6
1982	5.0	21.7
1983	4.9	21.3

Sources: U.S. Department of Health and Human Services, Vital Statistics of the United States 1982, Vol. III: Marriage and Divorce (Washington, D.C.: U.S. Government Printing Office), Tables 2-1 and 2-11; and The Statistical Abstract 1987, p. 80.

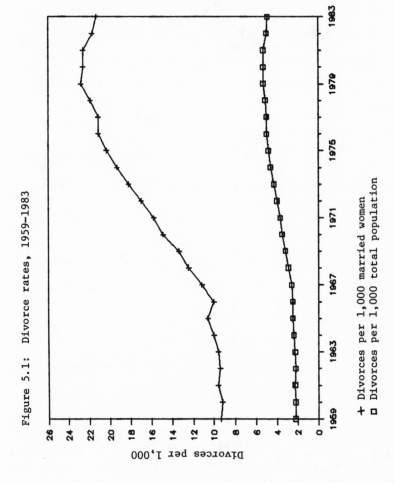

Figure 5.1: Divorce rates, 1959–1983

+ Divorces per 1,000 married women
□ Divorces per 1,000 total population

Source: Table 5.1

reflect growth in the nation's population. The number of divorces per 1,000 married women could mask a smaller base population if the size of the married population significantly declined.

Thus the model will employ the series reflecting the divorce rate among the population as a whole. This series clearly shows that divorce became more prevalent from the mid 1960s through the mid 1970s and has generally remained at relatively high rates through 1983.

III: The Data on the Composition of Growth

In the previous chapter the composition of growth was viewed in a framework of manufacturing versus the private services. That perspective will be maintained for the purposes of this model. The output per capita of each of these two sectors from 1959 to 1984 was provided in Table 4.8 and Figure 4.1. The third column presented the ratio of manufacturing output to the output of the private services. This variable reflects the relative strength of the two sectors and will be used in the model as an indicator of the composition of economic growth. This ratio peaked in 1966 and then generally declined through 1984.

IV: Inclusion of the Divorce Rate and the Structural
Ratio as Explanatory Variables

Do higher incidences of divorce and the increased
dominance of private services in the economy help explain
the relationship between growth and poverty reduction?
Econometric analysis can be employed to see whether
inclusion of the divorce and structure of growth factors
helps explain the impact of growth on the poverty rate.
Initially the following two models will be contrasted and
evaluated.

Model A:

$$\Delta PR = a + b \, (GNPpcg) \tag{1}$$

Model B:

$$\Delta PR = a + b \, (GNPpcg) \tag{2}$$

$$\text{where } b = c + d \, (DR) + e \, (ManQ/PSQ) \tag{3}$$

In its reduced form Model B becomes

$$\Delta PR = a + c \, (GNPpcg) + d \, (DR)(GNPpcg) + e \, (ManQ/PSQ)(GNPpcg) \tag{4}$$

For both models

$$
\begin{aligned}
PR &= \text{aggregate poverty rate;} \\
GNPpcg &= \text{real GNP per capita growth;} \\
DR &= \text{divorce rate per 1,000 total population;} \\
ManQ/PSQ &= \text{the ratio of manufacturing output to output} \\
&\quad \text{in private services.}
\end{aligned}
$$

In both of these models changes in the poverty rate depend upon per capita growth in GNP. However in Model A that relationship is constant over time and is represented by the value of the coefficient b. In contrast in Model B the value of the coefficient on GNP per capita growth is a function of the divorce rate and the structure of economic growth variable. The results for each Model are provided in Table 5.2.

Table 5.2:   Regression results for Models A and B

Model A

Variable	Coefficient	Estimate	T-statistic
Constant	a	0.167	0.89
GNPpcg	b	-0.005	-4.09*

Durbin-Watson = 0.96;
R-squared = 0.43.

Model B

Variable	Coefficient	Estimate	T-statistic
Constant	a	0.423	3.18*
GNPpcg	c	-0.009	-0.71
(DR)(GNPpcg)	d	0.003	3.63*
(ManQ/PSQ)(GNPpcg)	e	-0.015	-0.62

Durbin-Watson = 2.12;
R-squared = 0.78.

* = significant at 95% level of confidence.

For Model A the coefficient on (GNPpcg) has the expected negative sign and is statistically significant. For Model B the constant term and the divorce/growth interaction term are statistically significant. The R-squared for Model B is markedly larger than for Model A.

Another useful perspective on the difference between the two models is to contrast Model A in Equation (1) with the reduced form of Model B in Equation (4). In this light Model A can be viewed as a restricted form of Model B. That is, with the restrictions that coefficients d and e are equal to zero, Model B collapses into Model A.

The most critical econometric test pertinent to the task of supporting the posited theory is whether Model B has significantly greater explanatory power than Model A. In essence the question is: Does inclusion of the divorce and structure variables significantly help explain the impact of growth on the poverty rate? I will now demonstrate that Model B, in which the anti-poverty impact of growth depends on divorce and the structure of growth, is a significant improvement over Model A in which the impact of growth on poverty is not a function of the divorce and structure factors.

In general the F test can be employed to see whether the addition of a group of variables helps explain the behavior of the dependent variable.[1] The test statistic is

$$F = \frac{(ESSr - ESSur)/q}{ESSur/(N-k)} \qquad (5)$$

    where r denotes the restricted model,
        ur denotes the unrestricted model,

  and where ESS = error sum of squares;
             q = number of restrictions;
           (N-k) = degrees of freedom in the unrestricted
                   model.

Substitutions into Equation (5) yield the F value of 15.6.   Hence it is demonstrated at a 95 percent level of confidence that the addition of the group (of two) terms significantly adds to the explanatory power of the model. This result lends strong and critical support to the principal thesis that the anti-poverty impact of growth is affected by the divorce rate and the structure of economic growth.

V. The Model Specification and Results

The regression results of Model B indicated low t-statistics for the coefficients on (GNPpcg) and the interaction term [(GNPpcg)(ManQ/GNPpcg)]. These reflect the large standard errors associated with each parameter which in turn point to the possible problem of

---

[1]For a description of this joint test on several regression coefficients see Pindyck and Rubinfeld, 117-120.

multicollinearity. In fact, we must expect a high degree of correlation between these variables because, as was suggested in Chapter 4, manufacturing output is cyclically sensitive and as a result the (ManQ/PSQ) ratio is likely to increase when GNP per capita growth is high and decrease when GNP per capita growth is low. This expectation that there is high correlation between the growth variable and the growth/structure interaction variable is supported by the Pearson correlation coefficient of 0.996 between the two variables. Hence multicollinearity is apparent.

The problem of multicollinearity can be reduced by dropping a variable. A third model in which the (GNPpcg) variable is omitted will now be formally presented and contrasted to Model B. However, this new model must be statistically evaluated in terms of the impact of dropping a variable on the predictive ability of the model.

Model C:

Δ PR = a + b (GNPpcg)   (6)

   where b = d (DR) + e (ManQ/PSQ)   (7)

In its reduced form Model C becomes

Δ PR = a + d (DR)(GNPpcg) + e (ManQ/PSQ)(GNPpcg)   (8)

A comparison of Equations (3) and (7) shows that Models B and C differ only in that Model C has no intercept term in its specification of b, the coefficient on GNPpcg. As a consequence the reduced forms of the models differ in that in Model B, Equation (4), there is a GNPpcg term. In Model C, Equation (8) this term is absent. Also absent in Model C is the problem of multicollinearity previously discussed.

The results for Model C appear in Table 5.3. The results support the hypotheses that higher rates of divorce counter the anti-poverty effect of economic growth and that growth more heavily dominated by the private service industries leaves aggregate growth a less powerful anti-poverty weapon.

Table 5.3: Regression results for Model C

Variable	Coefficient	Estimate	T-statistic
Constant	a	0.434	3.34*
(DR)(GNPpcg)	d	0.002	5.18*
(ManQ/PSQ)(GNPpcg)	e	-0.031	-7.21*

Durbin-Watson = 2.08;
R-squared = 0.77.

 * = significant at 95% level of confidence.

The estimated coefficients can be substituted into Equation (7) to obtain estimates of the value of b, the coefficient on GNP per capita growth. These estimates, and the associated standard errors and t-statistics are provided in Table 5.4. After an initial period of a strengthened relationship, which corresponds to a relatively steady divorce rate and an increase in the manufacturing sector share of total output, the coefficient on GNP growth generally approached zero through the end of the study period. Interestingly, the values are significantly different from zero only in years 1960 through 1974. Beginning in 1975 we cannot say with confidence that the coefficient differed from zero.

Additionally, the null hypothesis that the coefficient in 1960 equals the coefficient in 1983 can be tested by evaluating the following test statistic:

$$t = \frac{b_{1960} - b_{1983}}{\sqrt{\left(SE_{b_{1960}}\right)^2 + \left(SE_{b_{1983}}\right)^2 + 2\ cov\ b_{1960}b_{1983}}}$$

assump cov = ∅

The value obtained equals −5.22, large enough to reject the null hypothesis and to assert with 95 percent confidence that there is a statistically significant difference in the value of these two coefficients. This result supports the hypothesis that the link between aggregate growth and poverty reduction has weakened over

Table 5.4:   Estimated sensitivity of the poverty rate to growth in GNP per capita

Year	Estimated b	Standard error	T-statistic
1960	-0.00975	0.00192	5.08*
1961	-0.00890	0.00184	4.84*
1962	-0.00975	0.00192	5.08*
1963	-0.01014	0.00200	5.07*
1964	-0.01021	0.00204	5.00*
1965	-0.01029	0.00208	4.95*
1966	-0.01060	0.00212	5.00*
1967	-0.00975	0.00204	4.78*
1968	-0.00906	0.00204	4.44*
1969	-0.00836	0.00204	4.10*
1970	-0.00643	0.00188	3.42*
1971	-0.00566	0.00184	3.07*
1972	-0.00558	0.00192	2.91*
1973	-0.00581	0.00204	2.85*
1974	-0.00419	0.00192	2.18*
1975	-0.00249	0.00176	1.41
1976	-0.00265	0.00184	1.44
1977	-0.00296	0.00188	1.57
1978	-0.00242	0.00184	1.31
1979	-0.00195	0.00184	1.06
1980	-0.00126	0.00172	0.73
1981	-0.00103	0.00172	0.60
1982	-0.00079	0.00160	0.49
1983	-0.00133	0.00164	0.81

* statistically significant at 95% level of confidence

the period and that economic growth has become a less viable anti-poverty weapon.

Finally, if we turn to the potential obstacle encountered by deleting the (GNPpcg) term, what can be said about the relative ability of Model C to explain changes in the poverty rate? That is, compared to Model B with its inclusion of the additional term, does Model C perform poorly? The F test can again be employed to test whether the inclusion of the intercept in Equation (3) significantly improves the explanatory power of the model. In this case Model C is the restricted model with the single restriction that in Equation (3) the coefficient c equals zero. Model B is again the unrestricted model.

Substitutions into Equation (5) yields the F value of 0.49, a value too small to be statistically significant. Consequently the inclusion of the intercept in Model B does not significantly enhance the explanatory power of the model. The intercept can be dropped and with it the problem of multicollinearity is diminished. For these reasons Model C is adopted as the model used to evaluate and predict the anti-poverty impact of economic growth.

VI: The Future Anti-poverty Impact of Economic Growth

The potential of aggregate economic growth as a remedy for modern U.S. aggregate poverty has been diminished by the increased incidence of divorce and by the shift in the sectoral composition of growth toward an enhanced role of private service output. Should the high rates of divorce continue and a similar composition of economic growth be maintained, aggregate economic growth will remain a less viable instrument for reducing the nation's poverty. To anticipate the future anti-poverty impact of economic growth we are required to anticipate future levels of divorce and the future composition of economic growth. For these purposes I will employ the expertise of specialists in those areas.

Sociologists recognize many factors which impact the rate of divorce. The list includes the age distribution of the population, the age at the time of marriage, the number of children in the family, the education attainment of the couple, the state of the economy, the labor market status of women, the degree of cohabitation outside of marriage, the rates of marriage and remarriage, and the level of social acceptance of divorce as a means for resolving serious marital difficulties. Because many of these factors are themselves hard to predict, the divorce rate is also difficult to anticipate.[2]

Nevertheless Glick and Lin have offered comments on the future of the divorce rate in the United States.[3] These comments followed a brief recounting of the overall trend of divorce. Namely that "the divorce rate actually rose by a factor of more than 17 during the period for which U.S. divorce statistics are available. Thus, the rate went up from only 0.3 per 1,000 population in 1867 to a peak of 5.3 per 1,000 population in 1979." Their study specifically stated that the rapid increase in the divorce rate in the 1960s and 1970s (illustrated in Table 5.1 and Figure 5.1 above) "constituted primarily an accentuation of the long-term upward trend in divorce."[4]

Glick and Lin offered the following prediction:

> The future trends in divorce and remarriage are not easy to predict with confidence, partly because the levels of the rates appear to have approached either a turning point toward higher levels or to have entered a period of relative stability. ... [I]t should not be surprising if the divorce rate were to continue to fluctuate

---

[2]Paul C. Glick and Sung-Ling Lin, "Recent Changes in Divorce and Remarriage," Journal of Marriage and the Family, 48, no. 4 (November, 1986), 737-747.

[3]Ibid.

[4]Ibid., 738 and 744.

moderately near the current level before reaching a period of relative stability.[5]

To predict the future anti-poverty impact of economic growth I will employ two divorce rates, i.e., a "high" rate and a "low" rate, in an effort to cover the range of probable outcomes. These rates are first, the 1979 peak value of 5.3 per 1,000 total population and second, the 1983 value of 4.9 that was the lowest value since the 1979 peak.

Predictions for the composition of economic growth were derived from a study prepared by Valerie A. Personick in which she "describes the trends of industry output and employment projected by the Bureau of Labor Statistics for the remainder of the 20th century."[6] Estimates were provided for "high," "moderate," and "low" average annual rates of change in manufacturing and the services industries. I employed Personick's varied growth rates to extrapolate from the previous output data (Table 4.8) the output levels for the year 2000. From these extrapolated output figures I obtained corresponding predictions for this study's variable which represents the composition of economic growth.

---

[5]Ibid., 744-5.

[6]Valerie A. Personick, "Projections 2000: Industry Output and Employment through the End of the Century," Monthly Labor Review, 110, no.9 (September, 1987), 30.

There was an incongruency between Personick's data and my data. My consideration of the service producing sectors excludes the government output, while Personick's estimate for the service industries included government output. According to Personick, among all of the service industries, government is the sector which is expected to experience the lowest percentage growth. Thus the inclusion of the government sector makes Personick's estimate of growth in the services lower than an estimate that would apply solely to the private services. However, an estimate applicable only to the private services is not available. Hence I will use Personick's estimate for growth in the services (including government) as a predictor for growth in the private services. The implication is that it will bias downward my predictions of growth in the private services, and consequently will bias upward my predictions of the ratio of manufacturing output to private services output. Since higher values of this ratio render growth more effective at remedying poverty, my final predictions on the anti-poverty effectiveness of economic growth can be considered optimistic or "best case."

Table 5.5 reports the estimates for the average annual rate of percentage change in manufacturing and the services under "low" growth and "high" growth scenarios.

Table 5.5:   Estimated values for the composition of
economic growth in the year 2000

Average annual rate of percentage change in output	Manufacturing	Services
"Low" growth	1.3	1.8
"High" growth	2.9	3.1

Corresponding
extrapolated
output levels

	Manufacturing	Services
"Low" growth	$2032	5222
"High" growth	2612	6397

	Corresponding ratio of manufacturing output to private services output
"Low" growth	0.39
"High" growth	0.41

Source: Derived from CITIBASE and Personick.

If economic growth is "low" then manufacturing is expected to grow at 1.3 percent per year and the services will increase at 1.8 percent per year, and if growth is "high" then the manufacturing and services growth will be 2.9 percent per year and 3.1 percent per year, respectively. Next the Table reports the corresponding extrapolated output levels for each sector under each growth scenario. For example, in Table 4.8 manufacturing output per capita in 1984 was $1653. Under the "low" assumption of an annual 1.3 percent growth rate, the manufacturing output level in the year 2000 will be $2032. After each sector's output was estimated under each growth pattern, the corresponding composition of growth variable was calculated. Thus under the "low" growth projection, the ratio of manufacturing output to private services output is expected to equal 0.39. Alternatively if the "high" growth pattern is realized, the ratio representing the composition of growth will equal 0.41.

These ratios indicate that under the "high" growth scenario, manufacturing is expected to perform better relative to the services than under the "low" growth outcome. Thus with "high" growth, the composition of growth is expected to make it more effective at fighting poverty. If, however, the economy experiences "low" growth, manufacturing will not do as well vis-a-vis the services. In this case the composition of growth will render growth less viable at remedying poverty.

Now we are ready to predict the anti-poverty impact of growth under these alternative scenarios of divorce and the composition of economic growth. The predictions are of the coefficient b in Equation (6), which indicates the responsiveness of the poverty rate to changes in GNP per capita. Large negative values indicate that growth will be more useful at remedying poverty. The results appear in Table 5.6.

As expected, a "high" divorce rate will reduce the responsiveness of the poverty rate to economic growth. This is evidenced by the numbers in the first row having smaller absolute values than the numbers in the second row. Also, a smaller value for the composition of growth variable will render economic growth less potent at reducing poverty. Consequently, the predictions in the right column indicate a lower anti-poverty impact of growth.

Finally these numbers are put into historic perspective in Figure 5.2. The Figure presents the previously obtained estimates of b over the 1960 to 1983 time period as indicated in Table 5.4. Also presented are the predicted values for the year 2000. The most

Table 5.6: Predictions of the sensitivity of the poverty
rate to growth in GNP per capita

| | Ratio of manufacturing output to private services output (corresponding to) | |
	0.41 ("High" growth)	0.39 ("Low" growth)
"High" divorce rate 5.3 percent	-0.00211	-0.00149
"Low" divorce rate 4.9 percent	-0.00291	-0.00229

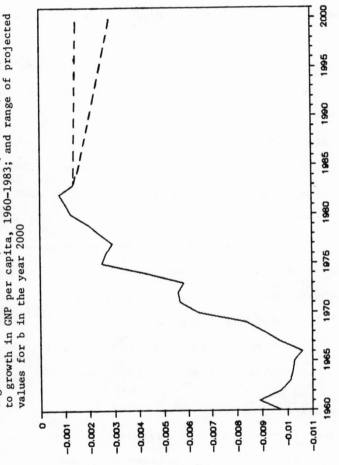

Figure 5.2: Estimated b, or sensitivity of the poverty rate
to growth in GNP per capita, 1960-1983; and range of projected
values for b in the year 2000

Sources: Tables 5.4 and 5.5

optimistic prediction, -0.00291, corresponds to the values of the mid 1970s, years in which the progress against poverty began to stagnate. (See Table I.1.) The great progress against poverty which occurred in the 1960s was associated with values three or more times larger than the most optimistic prediction. The remaining of the predicted values correspond to the values for the 1980s, a period of overall increase in the poverty rate.

In sum, the viability of economic growth as a remedy for official poverty has diminished since the early 1960s. This can be attributed to two factors: the increased rate of divorce and the shift of the economy away from the production of manufacturing and toward the production of private services. Given the current varied assumptions concerning the anticipated rates of divorce and the future composition of economic growth, entering the next century we can expect economic growth to remain a weakened instrument against poverty.

VII: Qualifications

I have reached these conclusions by making a number of potentially severe assumptions. These assumptions will now be reviewed.

First, in this dissertation I used the official U.S. Government definition of poverty. This gross measure of income has been criticized on many grounds.[7] Nonetheless it is a very commonly used poverty standard and it is the measure employed in each of the studies in the literature review that were conducted after these poverty data became available.

Second, I only include two factors which impact the anti-poverty effect of growth despite the likelihood that there are other significant factors. However the principal argument is that the relationship between growth and poverty reduction changes over time and for this purpose the consideration of only these two factors suffices. Furthermore, while these are likely not the only two factors which influence the relationship, they are put forth as very important factors.

Third, I assume that changes in the poverty rate of female-headed households, changes in the poverty rate of other headed households, and changes in the demographic mix between female-headed households and other headed households are independent. This seems a drastic

---

[7]For a complete history of the development of the U.S. Government definition of poverty, its strengths and its weaknesses, see: Sharon Oster, Elizabeth E. Lake, and Conchita Gene Oksman, The Definition of Poverty, Volume 1: A Review (Boulder: Westview Press, 1978).

assumption. However this assumption is needed in order to address the interesting and important issue of the extent to which the feminization of poverty was a demographic phenomenon and to what extent it was caused by relative changes in the poverty rates of men and women. Given that the orthodox theory suggests that the poverty rate of female-headed households should increase as more of the population moves into these households and that, in fact, this poverty rate decreased, I felt emboldened and went forward with assuming that the poverty rate must instead depend heavily on other factors besides the demographic composition.

Fourth, the poverty rates of other headed households are used to reflect the economic status of men in the same way that the poverty rates of female headed households are employed to reflect the economic status of women. This assumption is very problematic because other headed households often include women earners. I defend this assumption based on the recognition that the economic successes and failures of men do dramatically impact the poverty status of other headed households and because men's earnings are typically higher, men's incomes are more critical to the economic welfare of these households. Given the absence of alternative data I use these data accompanied by this qualification.

Fifth, as explained in the Appendix I superimpose data sets to get a series on the historic pattern of poor adult women and poor adult men. However I only use these data in a broad descriptive sense and they are not used to obtain regression results. Furthermore, the years of overlap in the data sources provide comparable numbers.

Appendix

From 1959 to 1973 the Bureau of the Census P-60 Series[1] provided data on persons below the poverty line by family status and sex of head. Estimates were provided for the numbers of poor male heads, poor female heads, and poor male and female unrelated individuals. I summed the number of poor male heads and the number of poor male unrelated individuals to obtain an estimate of poor adult males. The population of poor adult females consisted of poor female heads, poor female unrelated individuals, and wives of poor male heads. The number of wives was estimated for each year by multiplying the number of poor male heads by the percentage of male-headed households which in that year had a wife present, a statistic published in the Bureau of the Census P-20 Series.[2] It is acknowledged that this percentage may have differed among families above and below the poverty line thereby resulting in some inaccuracy. Additionally, some poor women are not represented in these estimates. Namely, related women

---

[1]U.S. Department of Commerce, Bureau of the Census, Current Population Report P-60 Series, Consumer Income.

[2]U.S. Department of Commerce, Bureau of the Census, Current Population Reports P-20 Series, Population Characteristics.

who live with the family, but who are neither the head nor the wife; for example, a grandmother. Finally, unrelated individuals in these tables included persons of 14 years of age and older, thereby including these young people in the author's estimates of the adult poor. While the magnitudes of the biases created by these difficulties are unknown, the biases created by each of the last two problems do work in opposition to one another. Overall the discrepancies are deemed likely not so large as to negate the very general conclusion of the exercise.

Concerning the Census estimates of 1969 through 1984, the women are 22 years old and older. While a younger cutoff was preferable, the published data were not consistent in age cohort divisions to allow an alternative and younger definition of "adult." That is, in some years the count was available for 18 and older, but in others the division began at age 16. However, in every year the population older than 21 was identified.

The two populations then in theory are not strictly identical. However, in the absence of more accurate data, these figures are held to be sufficient to buttress the general claim made in the text.

Bibliography

Aaron, Henry. "The Foundations of the 'War on Poverty'
      Re-examined." American Economic Review, 57
      (December, 1967), 1229-40.

Anderson, W. H. Locke.   "Trickling Down: The
      Relationship Between Economic Growth and the Extent
      of Poverty Among American Families." Quarterly
      Journal of Economics, 78 (November, 1964), 511-24.

Blau, Francine D. and Ferber, Marianne A.   The Economics
      of Women, Men and Work.   Englewood Cliffs, New
      Jersey: Printice-Hall, 1986.

Blau, Francine D. and Hendricks, Wallace E. "Occupational
      Segregation by Sex: Trends and Prospects." The
      Journal of Human Resources, 14, no. 2 (Spring,
      1979), 197-210.

Bluestone, Barry, and Harrison, Bennett.   The
      Deindustrialization of America.   New York: Basic
      Books, Inc., 1982.

Burgess, M. Elaine.   "Poverty and Dependency." Journal
      of Social Issues, 21 (January, 1965), 79-97.

Burnham, Linda,   "Has Poverty Been Feminized in Black
      America?" in For Crying Out Loud: Women and
      Poverty in the United States.   Edited by Rochelle
      Lefkowitz and Ann Whithorn.   New York: The Pilgrim
      Press, 1986.

CITIBASE: Citibank economic database [machine-readable
      magnetic data file].   1946-1984. New York, Citibank,
      N.A. 1978.

Corcoran, Mary; Duncan, Greg J.; Hill, Martha S.   "The
      Economic Fortunes of Women and Children: Lessons
      from the Panel Study of Income Dynamics."   In Women
      in Poverty.   Edited by Clare C. Novak and Myra H.
      Strober.   Chicago: The University of Chicago Press,
      1986.

Duncan, Greg J.; Coe, Richard D.; Corcoran, Mary E.;
    Hill, Martha S.: Hoffman, Saul D.; and Morgan,
    James N. Years of Poverty, Years of Plenty. Ann
    Arbor, Michigan: The University of Michigan, 1984.

Ehrenreich, Barbara and Piven, Frances Fox. "The
    Feminization of Poverty: When the 'Family-wage
    System Breaks Down." Dissent 1984, 162-169.

Galbraith, John Kenneth. The Affluent Society. Boston:
    Houghton Mifflin Company, 1958.

Gallaway, Lowell E. "The Foundations of the 'War on
    Poverty.'" American Economic Review, 55 (March,
    1965), 123-31.

_____. "The Foundations of the 'War on Poverty':
    Reply." American Economic Review, 57 (December,
    1967), 1241-43.

Glick, Paul C. and Lin, Sung-Ling. "Recent Changes in
    Divorce and Remarriage." Journal of Marriage and
    the Family, 48, no. 4, (November, 1986), 737-747.

Gottschalk, Peter and Danziger, Sheldon. "Changes in
    Poverty, 1967-1982: Methodological Issues and
    Evidence." Discussion Paper No. 737-83, Institute
    for Research on Poverty, 1983.

_____. "A Framework for Evaluating the Effects of
    Economic Growth and Transfers on Poverty." American
    Economic Review, 75 (March, 1985), 153-61.

_____. "Do Rising Tides Lift All Boats? The Impact of
    Secular and Cyclical Changes on Poverty." American
    Economic Review, 76, No. 2 (May, 1986), 405-10.

Harrington, Michael. The Other America: Poverty in the
    United States. New York: Macmillan Company, 1962.

_____. The New American Poverty. New York: Holt,
    Rinehart and Winston, 1984.

Hirsch, Barry T. "Poverty and Economic Growth: Has
    Trickle Down Petered Out?" Economic Inquiry, 18
    (January, 1980), 151-58.

Hoffman, Saul and Holmes, John. "Husbands, Wives, and Divorce." Five Thousand American Families -Patterns Economic Progress. Edited by Greg J. Duncan and James N. Morgan. Ann Arbor, Michigan: Institute For Social Research, The University of Michigan, 1976.

Kutsher, Ronald E., and Personick, Valerie A. "Deindustrialization and the Shift to Services." Monthly Labor Review, (June, 1986), 3-13.

Lampman, Robert J. The Low Income Population and Economic Growth. Study Paper No. 12, Joint Economic Committee, 86th Congress of the United States, 1st Session, December 16, 1959.

Mellor, Earl F. and Stamas, George D. "Usual Weekly Earnings: Another Look at Intergroup Differences and Basic Trends." Monthly Labor Review (April, 1982), 15-24.

Miller, S. M., and Tomaskovic-Dewey, Donald. Recapitalizing America. Boston: Routledge and Kegan Paul, 1986.

Murray, Charles A. "The Two Wars Against Poverty." The Public Interest, 69 (Fall, 1982), 3-16.

New Jersey Supreme Court Task Force on Women in the Courts. "The First Year Report of the New Jersey Supreme Court Task Force on Women in the Courts - June 1984." Women's Rights Law Reporter, vol. 9, no.2 (Spring, 1986).

Orshansky, Mollie. "How Poverty is Measured." Monthly Labor Review, 92, no.2 (February, 1969) 37-41.

Oster, Sharon M.; Lake, Elizabeth E.; and Oksman, Conchita Gene. The Definition and Measurement of Poverty, Volume 1: A Review. Boulder: Westview Press, 1978.

Pearce, Diana. "The Feminization of Poverty: Women, Work, and Welfare." Urban and Social Change Review, 11, no. 1 (February, 1978), 28-36.

Perl, Lewis J. and Solnick, Loren M. "A Note on 'Trickling Down.'" Quarterly Journal of Economics, 85 (February, 1971), 171-78.

Personick, Valerie A. "Projections 2000: Industry Output and Employment through the End of the Century." Monthly Labor Review, 110, no. 9 (September, 1987), 30-45.

Pindyck, Robert S. and Rubinfeld, Daniel L. Econometric Models and Economic Forecasts. Second edition. New York: McGraw-Hill Book Company, 1981.

Reskin, Barbara F. and Hartmann, Heidi I. Women's Work, Men's Work: Sex Segregation on the Job. Washington, D.C.: National Academy Press, 1986.

Rytina, Nancy F. "Earnings of Men and Women: A Look at Specific Occupations." Monthly Labor Review, (April, 1982), 25-31.

Rytina, Nancy F. and Bianchi, Suzanne M. "Occupational Reclassification and Changes in Distribution by Gender." Monthly Labor Review, (March, 1984), 11-17.

Sekscenski, Edward. "Job Tenure Declines as Work Force Changes." Monthly Labor Review, 102, no. 12, (December, 1979), 48-50.

Smith, Adam. The Wealth of Nations. Books I-III. New York: Penguin Books, 1970.

Smith, Joan. "The Paradox of Women's Poverty: Wage-earning Women and Economic Transformation." In Women and Poverty. Edited by Clare C. Novak and Myra H. Strober. Chicago: The University of Chicago Press, 1986.

Smith, Shirley J. "Work Experience of the Labor Force During 1985." Monthly Labor Review, 110, no. 4 (April, 1987), 40-44.

Sparr, Pamela. "Reevaluating Feminist Economics: 'Feminization of Poverty' Ignored Key Issues." Dollars and Sense, no. 99, (September, 1984).

Stallard, Karen; Ehrenreich, Barbara; and Sklar, Holly. Poverty in the American Dream: Women and Children First. South End Press, 1983.

Stockman, David. _The Triumph of Politics: How the Reagan Revolution Failed_. New York: Harper & Row, Publishers, 1986.

Thornton, James R.; Agnello, Richard J.; and Link, Charles R. "Poverty and Economic Growth: Trickle Down Peters Out." _Economic Inquiry_, 16 (July, 1978), 385-94.

Thornton, James R.; Agnello, Richard J.; and Link, Charles R. "Poverty and Economic Growth: Trickle Down Has Petered Out." _Economic Inquiry_, 18, (January, 1980) 159-63.

U.S. Department of Commerce, Bureau of the Census. Current Population Reports P-20 Series. _Population Characteristics_. Washington, D.C.: Government Printing Office.

U.S. Department of Commerce, Bureau of the Census. Current Population Reports P-60 Series. _Consumer Income_, various issues. Washington, D.C.: Government Printing Office.

U.S. Department of Commerce, Bureau of the Census. _Statistical Abstract of the United States 1987_. Washington, D.C.: Government Printing Office, 1986.

U.S. Department of Health and Human Services. _Vital Statistics of the United States 1982_. Vol. III: _Marriage and Divorce_. Washington, D.C.: U.S. Government Printing Office.

U.S. Department of Labor, Bureau of Labor Statistics. _Employment and Earnings_, various issues. Washington, D.C.: U.S. Government Printing Office.

U.S. Department of Labor, Bureau of Labor Statistics. _Monthly Labor Review_, (March, 1987).

U.S. Department of Labor, Women's Bureau. _Time of Change: 1983 Handbook on Women Workers_. Bulletin 298. Washington, D.C.: U.S. Department of Labor, 1983.

Urquhart, Michael. "The Employment Shift to Services: Where Did It Come From?" _Monthly Labor Review_, (April, 1984), 15-22.

Weitzman, Lenore J. The Divorce Revolution: The
     Unexpected Consequences for Women and Children in
     America. New York: The Free Press, 1985.

_____. "The Economics of Divorce: Social and Economic
     Consequences of Property, Alimony, and Child Support
     Awards." UCLA Law Review, 28 (August, 1981), 1181-
     1268.